HANDCRAFT YOUR OWN SHOES AND BOOTS

A Step-By-Step Guide To Making Artisan

All Leather Shoes And Boots At Home

Neda Hussain

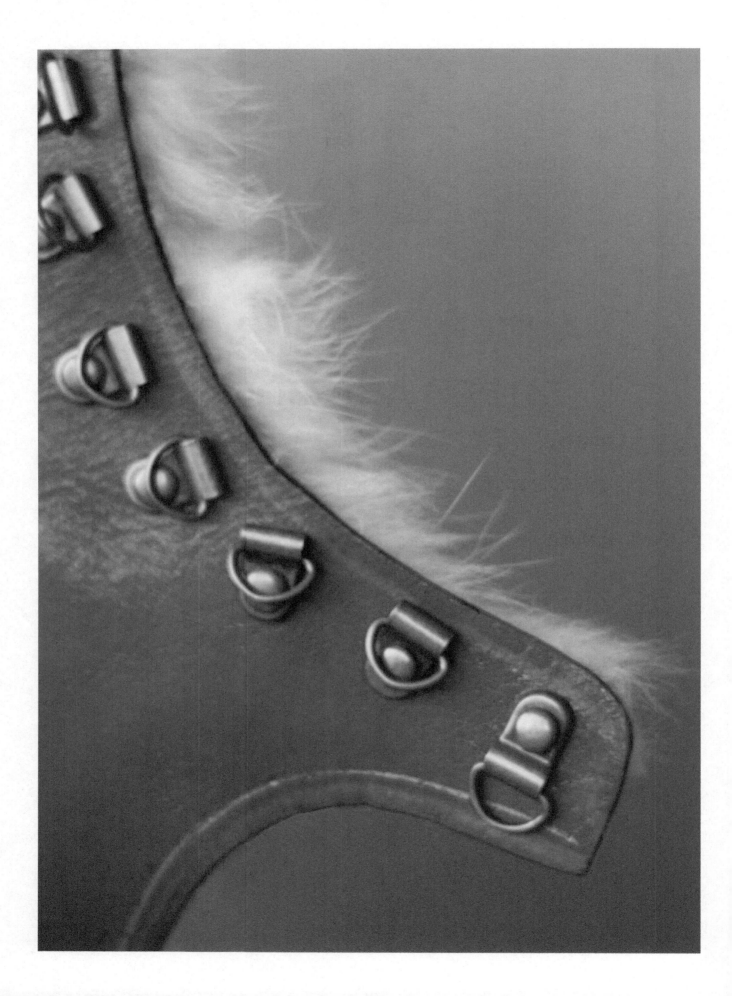

Contents

Introduction   7

About Neda   11

How To Use This Book   12

What kind of shoes can you make with this book?   15

1 Equipment   19

Essential Tools   19

Shoe Lasts   30

Materials   41

Leather Decorating Tools   55

2 Basic Techniques   56

Pattern Making   56

Cutting Out Leather   73

Dyeing Leather   76

Skiving   78

Making Toe Puffs and Heel Stiffeners   80

Lining Your Shoes   86

Setting Metal Eyelets   90

Hand Stitching   93

Constructing The Upper   102

Lasting   112

Attaching The Outsole   122

Attaching Heels   133

Protecting Leather Soles   133

Edge Finishing Soles   136

Cracking The Last   142

Caring For Your Shoes   144

3 The Projects   146

The Derby Shoe   148

Variation Of The Pattern   178

8-Eyelet Boots   182

14-Eyelet Boots   204

Half Bellows Tongue   228

Suppliers   241

Feedback   245

Sandal Making Book   246

Introduction

You are about to embark on a journey to become the maker of fantastic shoes and boots. Footwear is full of character that can not be bought in any shop.

Very few people make their own shoes. Shoemaking is generally perceived as too challenging for people to do at home, involving heavy machinery and several years of professional training.

Let me assure you there is a way we can make awesome shoes at home for fun and as a hobby using just our hands and a few tools. Yes, you have to invest in tools and a pair of lasts but remember you can use these over and over again, and the joy you feel making your own shoes is priceless.

Don't get me wrong, I am not saying it is easy. There definitely is a learning curve involved in this. But after you made your first pair of shoes or boots, the second pair will be so much easier.

Once I started making my own footwear, I never looked back. I have no interest at all in shoe shops. Nothing I can buy could ever be as beautiful as what I have made, even with little mistakes here and there.

Most factory-made shoes are filled with significant plastic components and do not last long, ending their short lives in a dump.

By contrast, when you make your shoes, you choose the material using the best possible ingredients to make them long-lasting. Furthermore, you can repair them yourself if needed.

On the following pages, you will learn how to be the artist and the technician, the designer and the maker of your shoes.

Please always remember to allow yourself to be a beginner. No one starts off being excellent. Following the instructions in this book, you will become the maker of great shoes and boots.

If you feel overwhelmed when leafing through this book, please do not give up. You can always start small by making sandals to gain confidence and develop your skills further when ready.

The most visited post on my blog is the first one I published in 2016 about how I started making boots. It was just intended as an inspirational post. I had not yet decided what to focus on: making clothes or jewellery, leather-work in general or shoemaking.

Over time it became clear that most people coming to my blog were interested in shoemaking. I got a lot of requests for a tutorial, so this book is my answer. I published it as an eBook at the end of 2020 on my website Second Skin Blog. It is still available there for purchase. Meanwhile, I learned how to self-publish printed books using Amazon as the print-on-demand service, so here it is for all of you who asked me for a paper version.

I am sharing all my knowledge in this book, hoping more people will be inspired to make their own shoes.

Let's empower ourselves to make almost anything we need eliminating our dependency on cheap factory products and exploiting no one!

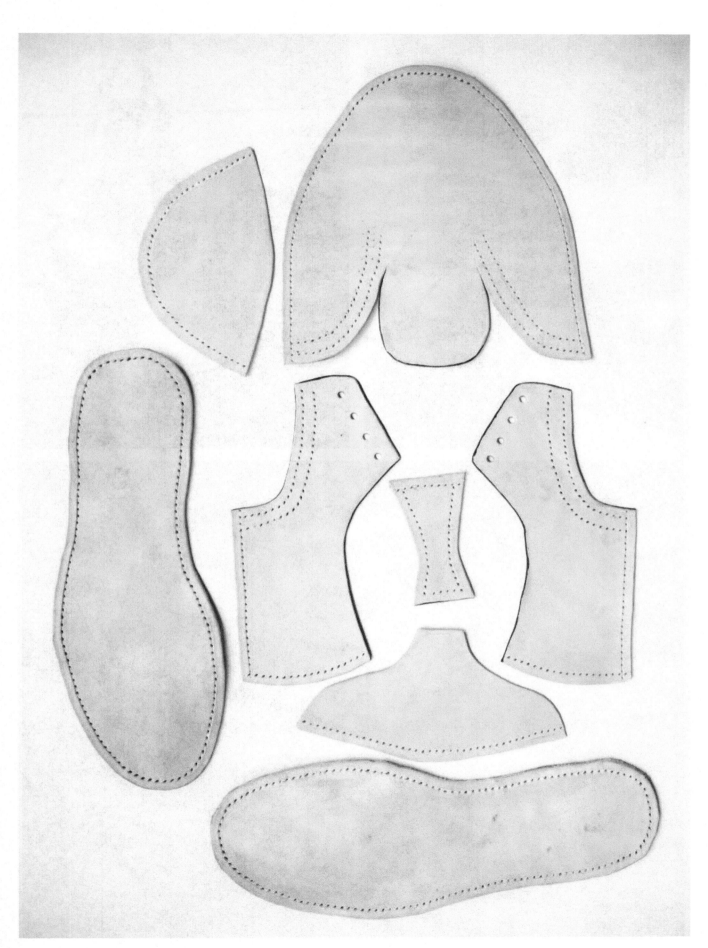

About Neda

I live a simple life infused with art and craft, making and creating whenever I'm not needed elsewhere. I also love growing my own food (and lots of flowers too).

For two decades, I lived the globetrotter life while working as a Social Anthropologist in Africa, Asia and South America. My life changed completely when I had children and decided to stay home with them. I discovered my love for crafts and working with my hands.

I have been living in England for quite a while now, collecting tools, cameras, instruments, fabrics and art supplies. Moving around is not so easy anymore.

Shoemaking is one of my favourite crafts, which I have been practising for over 10 years. I also wrote a book on making your own sandals which you can find as a downloadable eBook on my blog.

Follow me on Instagram

www.instagram.com/secondskinblog

or visit my blog: www.secondskinblog.com

How to use this book

The first section of this book describes the equipment you need to start making shoes. The second section covers the pattern-making process and the techniques I use to construct a shoe.

The third section explains how to make shoes and boots from start to finish, referring back to the previous chapters when necessary.

At the back of the book is a list of online suppliers from which you can source the necessary equipment. While I only cover the English-speaking countries, where most of the buyers of my eBook How To Make Unique Leather Sandals come from, all the shops mentioned sell worldwide.

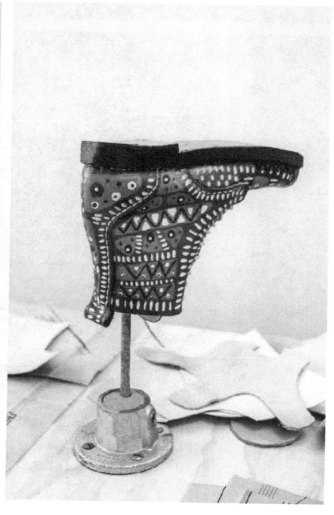

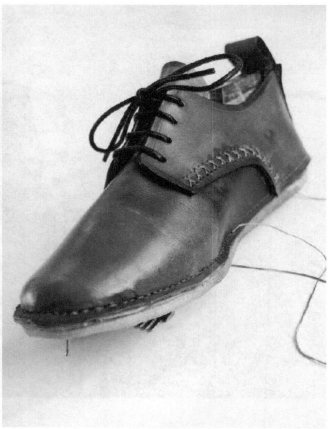

What kind of shoes can you make with this book?

Shoes can be made using different construction techniques: hand welted, cemented, Blake or Bologna, to mention just a few. In this book, I focus on the stitch-down construction. I think it is the perfect construction method for those who want to make shoes at home that look professional without needing a fully equipped shoemaker's workshop.

Any low-heeled shoe style can be made using the stitch-down construction, like Desert Boots, heavy boots, hiking boots, lightweight casuals of all kinds, renaissance-style shoes and children's shoes. Brands that use this construction method are Conker, Green Shoes and the shoemaker Ruth Emily Davey.

Unique about the stitch-down construction is that instead of the upper being tucked under the sole and sewn to or glued to the insole, the upper is turned out, enabling the maker to easily hand stitch the upper to the soles.

Stitch-down does not require a heavy walking foot sewing machine; all the work can be done by hand. In addition, this construction lends itself easily to water-based, solvent-free adhesives eliminating exposure to harmful fumes.

In this book, I show how to make Derby-style shoes. Unlike an Oxford-style shoe, the Derby has open lacing, meaning that quarters are stitched on top of the vamp. The tongue is cut as part of the vamp. There is no seam between the tongue and the front of the shoe. There are quite a few variations of this style: from five to one pair of eyelets and Derby boots from ankle to knee height.

The shoes in this book are made entirely of vegetable-tanned leather. I use a cow or calf hide to make the uppers and line them with soft calf or goat leather to make them highly durable. The uppers are sewn to thick and soft leather midsoles so that your unique footprints will embed into them.

The outer soles are leather too. An all-leather sole will feel better and better over time because it will begin to mould and compress to the contours of your foot so that it feels well-secured and cushioned. No one else can comfortably wear your shoes at that point. And the great news is they will stay just as comfortable for their entire life.

The healthiest shoes we can wear mimic barefoot walking. So I don't use any cushioning or other supports for the foot as these can lead to your foot muscles becoming weak as the padding inside the shoe does all of the work instead of your foot muscles.

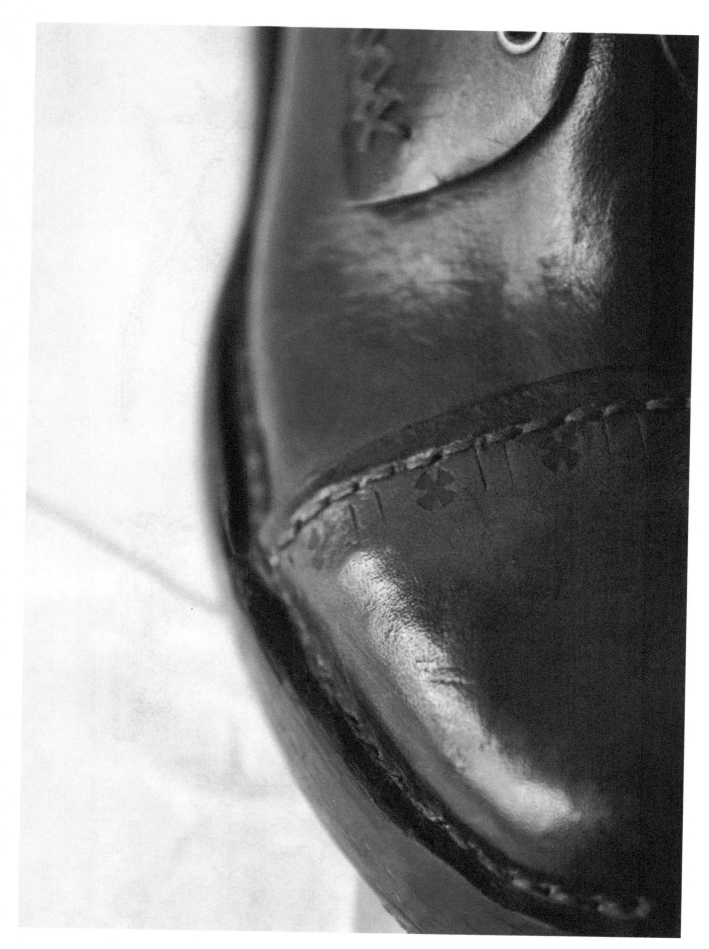

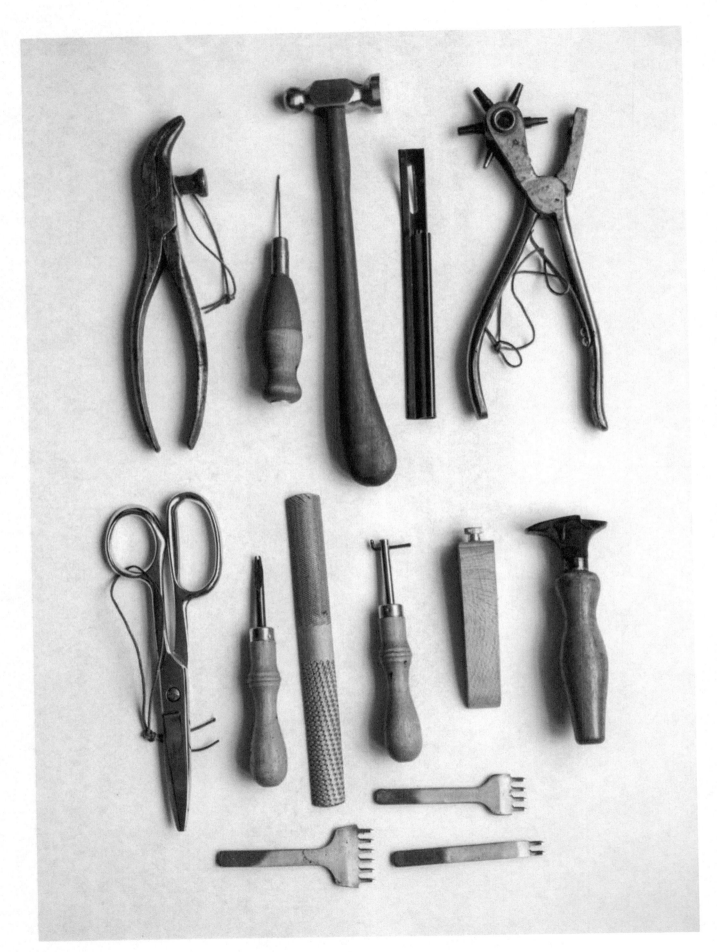

Equipment

Essential Tools

If you are a leather crafter, you probably have many of the tools listed here in your possession already. If not, don't worry. You can find most tools reasonably priced. Lasts will be the most costly item you will need. It is worth searching for second-hand or vintage ones for a fraction of the cost of new ones.

While it is great to work with the best tools available, to start with, cheaper ones will do. You can always replace them later on when you are sure you want to continue on this journey.

I recommend getting a good quality revolving hole punch and good leather shears. The cheaper ones may not punch or cut as well through thick midsole leather.

In the following pages, I list all the tools needed to make the shoes in this book.

Tools for cutting

Leather shears: Good leather shears cut through leather up to 4mm thickness without straining the hands.

A **utility knife** for cutting thick leather and soles. It has a replaceable blade feature and so does not need sharpening. You will also need blades because only very sharp knives will cut well. If you want to upgrade one day, you could check out a Tina Shoemaker's knife. It is razor-sharp and stays that way for a long time.

A **self-healing mat** for cutting soles and protecting your work table.

Leather shears

Utility knife

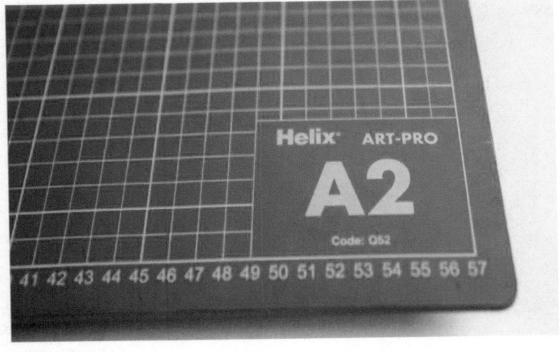

Self healing mat

Tools for punching holes

Revolving punch pliers are used to punch holes into the leather for stitching and punching eyelets.

Diamond chisel stitching punch kit with 6mm spacing between each tooth. They make very even diamond-shaped stitching holes.

A **mallet** to use with the chisels.

Revolving punch pliers

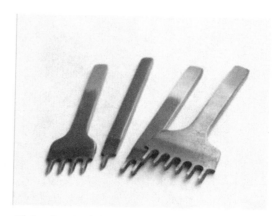

Chisel stitching punches

Mallet

Tools for stitching

A **stitching awl and needles** for making lock stitches. Stitches made with the awl can be compared to those a sewing machine would make.

Saddle stitching needles, you will need two for stitching the quarters back seam. Easy thread needles could also be used.

A **grooving tool** to create a channel into which the stitches are set. It protects the stitches from wear as they are embedded rather than sitting on the leather.

Stitching awl

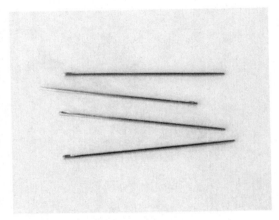

Saddle stitching needles

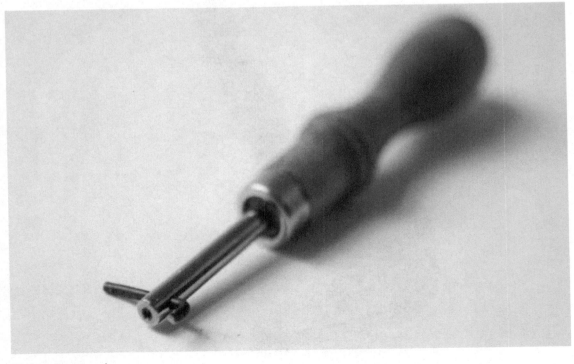

Grooving tool

Tools for skiving

A **skiving tool** is a special knife for removing bulk when turning or joining layers of leather. There are many different types of skiving knives available. The good ones can be expensive.

The skiving tool I am showing here is inexpensive and works fine if you change the blade frequently. They do not last long. Get a stash of them when you buy the tool.

If you want to upgrade one day or get something better straight away, a skiving knife by Tina or a Barnsley knife with a curved blade would be good choices. These need sharpening too from time to time.

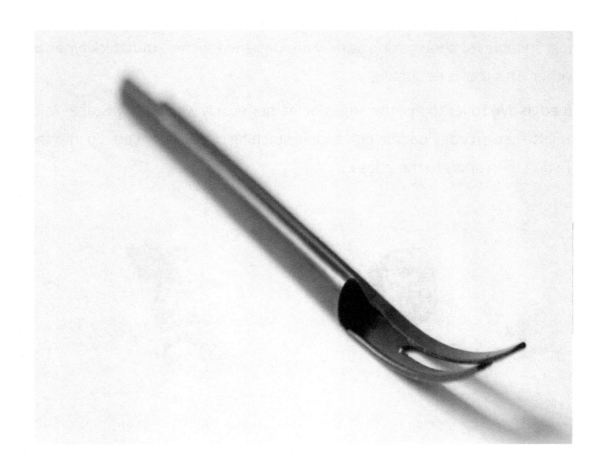

Tools for edge finishing

A **sanding block** to smooth the edges of cut leather. Good quality sandpaper is essential here (I use 80,120, 240, 400 and 800 grit).

A **shoemaker's rasp** for shaping soles and heels and blending

the layers of leather together to make one surface. Although you can use a woodworking rasp, a shoemaker's one will give better results.

A **glass slicker** for smoothing out the flesh side of leather and also for burnishing the edges of the soles. It is an optional tool.

A **wooden edge slicker** for burnishing the edges of cut leather.

An **edging iron** is designed to set the sole edges and give them a straight, solid and even surface. The iron is warmed over a flame and glided over the heel and sole edge as it burnishes wax into the surface.

An **edge beveler** to round off the edges of the leather. Size 1 or 2 are the most suitable for shoemaking as they are designed for 1 - 2mm thick types of leather. This tool is optional.

An **edge dye roller** to dye the edges of leather evenly with little wastage. You can also use an edge paddle or a saddle stitching needle that you dip into the dye and then apply to the edges.

Wooden sanding block

Sanding block with sandpaper

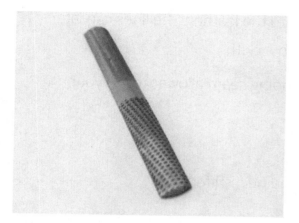

Shoemaker's rasp

Glass slicker

Wooden edge slicker

Edge iron

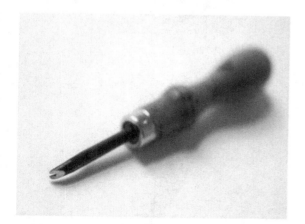

Edge beveler

Edge dye roller

Tools for pattern making

Flexible ruler, not absolutely necessary, but nice to have.

A **measuring tape**, if you are not familiar with the metric measuring system I use in this book, I recommend getting a measuring tape with both metric and imperial measurements.

A **silver pen** to mark the pattern pieces onto the leather. The lines can later be removed by just rubbing over them with a cloth.

A **compass or wing divider** to help with adding seam allowances to your paper patterns.

A **craft knife** for cutting into patterns.

Tracing paper is for designing toe puffs and heel stiffeners.

180° Protractor if you want to make high-rise boots (more than 8 pairs of eyelets).

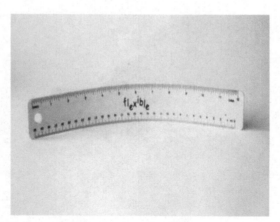

Flexible ruler

Measuring tape

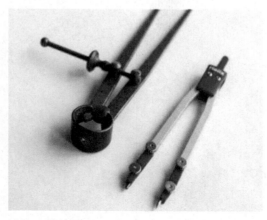

Wing Divider / Compass

Craft knife

Tools for lasting

Lasting pliers to grip the upper and stretch it into place over the last. They can also be used as a hammer to pound in nails. Lasting pliers are expensive new, I bought my vintage on eBay.

The **lasting jack/pole** removes the shoe from the last. They are costly, so try to make your own. I describe how on the next page. A lasting jack must be screwed onto a worktable. This means you have to drill into it. You could also fasten it to a wooden board big enough to sit on to have a counterweight when cracking the last.

Steel last hooks and hook prickers are also available. They are used by commercial shoemakers but work only for shoes.

You can use a metal pin like the one shown below to remove shoes from lasts, I show how it can be done in the chapter on making Derby boots.

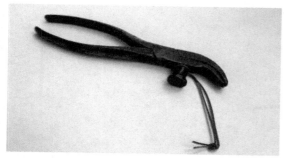

Lasting pliers

Metal pin

Lasting jack

Hot to make a lasting pole

Take your last to a DIY store and try to find a bolt that fits well into the hole on top of the last. It has to be 20 - 30 cm long, depending on the length of boots you want to make. You will also need a fitting nut.

Screw the bolt to a workbench or a piece of wood big enough for you to stand on. Use your own weight and leverage to crack the last hinge. Without a bench, you will have to get creative! But the lasting pole needs to be attached to something, even if it is portable.

Other useful tools

A **glass shard** is one of the best tools in shoemaking and is free! It is used for scraping and smoothing the surface of the sole edges. The glass used for picture frames about 2-3 mm thick works well for this purpose though any broken glass that is not too thin can be utilised. Ideally, the shard has an outward curve. I use any glass that broke in the house it works too.

A **cobblers anvil** for sole and heel work, hammering in nails, segs or hobnails.

An **eyelet setting kit** for leather, I use a flower punch for setting eyelets.

Cobblers anvil

Flower punch

Nail puller for lasting and pulling out misplaced nails.

Hammer, used for driving tacks and heel nails, adhering cemented parts together, tapping over hand stitching etc. If you are getting a hammer, you could try to find a cobbler's hammer (also called a French hammer).

They can be found vintage or second-hand. They look different from the one I am showing here. This is the one I had in the house so I am using it and it is fine as well.

Shoe Lasts

There is a saying in shoemaking that the last comes first. It is the soul of a shoe and the form the shoe is built on. The last dictates the style, the heel height, the size and the fit of the shoe.

The last is not a cast of a foot– it is the room you need inside the shoe to feel comfortable wearing it. The pattern for the lasted shoe is based on the outside measurements of the last in numerous places.

Lasts come in many styles and sizes, depending on the exact job they are designed for. Common variations include simple one-size lasts used for repairing soles and heels, plastic ones used in modern mass production, and custom-made ones used for bespoke footwear.

Shoe lasts are designed for a particular heel height, toe shape, and type of footwear like pumps, moccasins, shoes with laces, boots with zippers, boots without any fastening, sandals etc. There are men's, women's and children's lasts. Many shoe styles can be made on one pair of lasts, but the toe shape and heel height will be the same for all the shoes. The toe shapes of lasts can be changed. I will describe how in the following pages.

Bespoke shoemakers hand carve lasts from a block of dried Beechwood or Hornbeam. They integrate the shapes and measurements of the future wearer's foot so the shoes made on them will always fit perfectly.

There are last-making courses that teach the art of carving a wooden block into a last, which might be worth considering if you want to take shoemaking further.

Luckily, you can adapt existing lasts to the needs of your feet with a few add-ons, which I will explain later in the chapter.

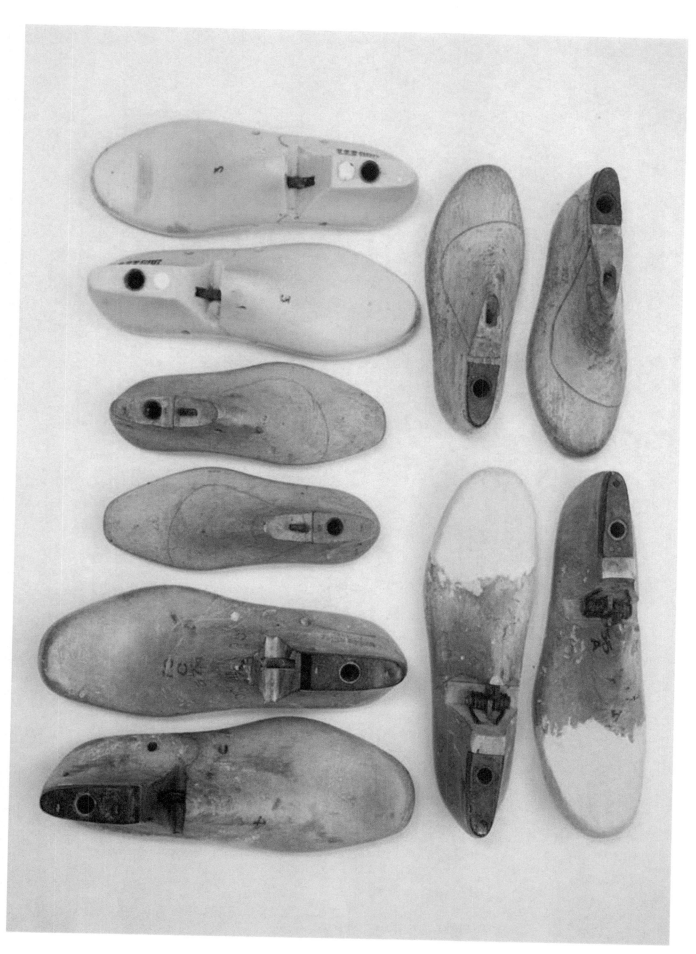

To make Derby shoes and boots, you will need lasts designed for lace-up shoes. Make sure the lasts are **hinged,** not solid. Those are for pattern design and open-back shoes like mules only. When researching this book on the Internet, I found several people asking how to get their shoes off the last. They used solid lasts that can not be removed from the shoe, other than slicing the shoe off.

You must select the correct last size lengthwise. The width can later be altered if necessary for fit. New lasts are sold in shoe sizes.

In contrast, if you buy vintage lasts, the size is often not clearly marked. In that case, you have to measure the length of the last and that of your foot. The correct last length is your foot length plus 1.5 - 2 cm.

Also, look at the shape of the last, especially the toe shape. The traditional shoe shape is the rounded toe which is spacious and very comfortable. They are the ones I am using in this book and are perfect for Derby shoes and boots. Other toe shapes are oval, almond and square-shaped. These lasts are used for Oxford-style shoes. Heel height has to be considered too. For beginning shoemakers, a last with a low heel is best (1-2cm).

Low-cost second-hand or vintage shoe lasts can sometimes be found on eBay or Etsy. The advantage of buying new lasts is that you can communicate with the shops selling them, explaining exactly what kind you want. Last shops sometimes offer the service that you can send them a drawing of your foot shape or a print and some measurements (like foot girth). They then find the most suitable last for your feet.

This is especially useful for people who have wide feet. You can alter a standard last to change its width. Although it is best if you have lasts that are just right for your feet.

Boots can be made on a shoe last, but not the other way around. If you made shoes on boot lasts, you would get very roomy heels. If you are sure you only want to make boots, you could get boot lasts. Make sure the boot lasts are made for lace-up boots, not slip-in, which are designed differently.

You can also have lasts made just for you. Your feet will be measured and lasts created to these exact measurements. Yes, it is a pricey option. Springline in the UK offers this service.

The following diagrams show how to best measure your feet. The length is measured from heel to longest toe.

The girth of your foot is the widest part of your feet (shown as A in the photo), and the arch is the highest part of the foot (B).

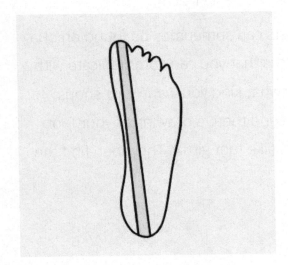
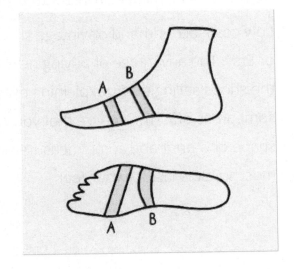

Altering a shoe last for boot making

Ideally, you would have lasts designed for lace-up boot making, but they are harder to find, at least second-hand.

If you only have shoemaking lasts, you can use them for making boots. For best results, you could add some fittings to the lasts.

My workaround is to nail or glue a piece of leather onto the cone and another piece onto the heel. It is not absolutely necessary, but I find it holds up the boot while sewing it all together and prevents the leather uppers from collapsing while working on the boot.

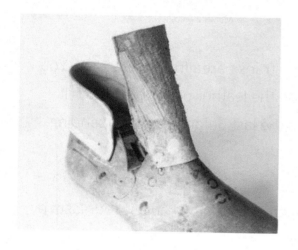 

Soak a piece of leather (about 2mm thick) in water for 1 minute. Next, skive it flat where it meets the last, there has to be a smooth transition from last to leather piece.

Use small tacks to attach it to the last or glue it on.

Do the same for the heel area. Then let it dry. It will transform into a stiff form better suited for boot making.

Changing the toe shape of a last

If you bought vintage lasts that have a toe shape you don't like, you could change it using epoxy clay. It holds onto the wood well and dries hard after a short time.

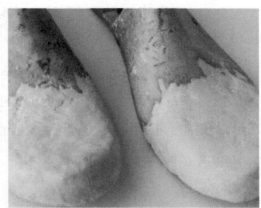

The challenge here is to get the toe shapes of both lasts as identical as possible. Once you are satisfied with the new toe shapes, let the clay dry for 1 hour.

Then sand the clay surface to smoothen it out. Pay special attention to the transit area from clay to last. You don't want any bumps which would show on the leather once you stretch it over the last. The photo on the right shows the last before and after sanding.

Changing the last to fit your feet

If you have wider than standard feet or a high arch you can adjust your lasts by attaching veg-tan leather patches at certain points.

In case you are buying new lasts, I do recommend communicating with the last supplier, so they can find the right last width for your feet.

However, if you bought second-hand lasts and want to use them, you can widen them with veg-tanned leather patches or wrap them with one piece of soft leather if you need more width all around.

Take the measurement for the girth and/or arch of your feet to determine what thickness has to be added to the last. Veg-tan leather becomes very soft when wet, so it can be easily sculpted around the form of the last. You can also layer the leather if more volume is needed.

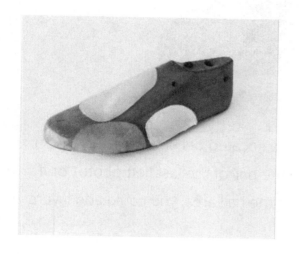 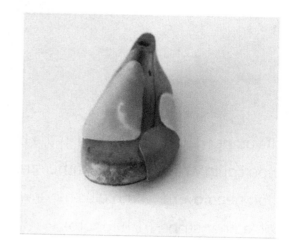

Renia 315 works well to attach the leather to the lasts. Once dry, the leather add-ons become solid. The leather patches have to be skived all around the edges to achieve a smooth transition from last to leather. You can additionally sand them once glued onto the lasts, so leather and last become one.

If you need more width around the last, you could wrap the front part with just one piece of leather. The advantage of this method is that the shape of the last is not changed, and there is less skiving to do (just the top part).

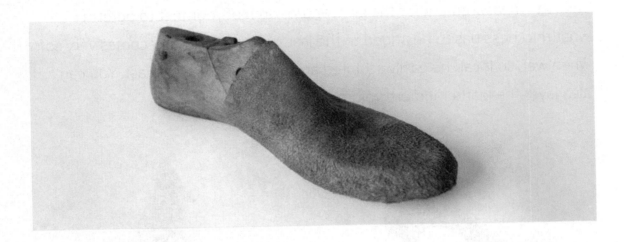

If you need additional room in the ball area (located between toes and arch), you could wrap a strip of leather around the ball of the last (left photo), or if you need overall width plus more width in the ball area, you could add layers of leather strips. (right photo).

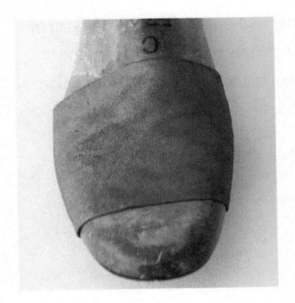

Leather

I use vegetable-tanned leather (veg-tan) for all my leather projects, as it is more environmentally friendly than chrome-tanned leather and can be dyed, tooled or painted easily.

Shoes made from veg-tan leather absorb moisture, so your feet stay dry and smell good even after years of wear. The tannins in veg-tan leather kill mould, fungus and mildew, creating a healthy environment for your feet. Furthermore, veg-tan leather is hard-wearing and develops a rich natural patina as time passes by.

It is called "vegetable" because of the materials used in the tanning process, like tree bark, leaves, wood, fruits and roots. Vegetable tanning is one of the oldest methods of tanning known to man. It takes several months to complete the veg-tan process.

Chrome-tanned leather is tanned using chromium and other harsh chemicals. Chrome is very toxic and environmentally damaging, and people working in tanning factories, mostly in developing countries, suffer serious health problems.

The tanning is completed much quicker, typically in a matter of days, making chrome-tanned leather a lot cheaper than veg-tan leather. 90% of all leather products are made from chrome-tanned leather, and 95% of all shoe leather.

While veg-tan leather costs more, you get value for your money. Some of the best veg-tan leathers for shoemaking come from small Italian tanneries that produce high-quality leather with a low ecological impact.

Try to buy veg-tan leather that is described as leather suitable for shoemaking with a soft or medium temper. It is tanned in the same way, but animal fat is added at some point in the process, which makes it mouldable. You can use stiffer veg-tan leather, but for the beginning, the softer shoe leather is easier to work with.

Make sure you buy full-grain leather, not corrected and sanded like top grain and "premium" leathers are. These thinned leathers might be cheaper and look and feel alright for a while, but they can not breathe as the surface has been squashed flat, so they will not last long or age well.

Leather is usually sold as hides. You can often choose between whole and half hides. Several pairs of shoes can be made with these hides. They are more economical than buying smaller pieces.

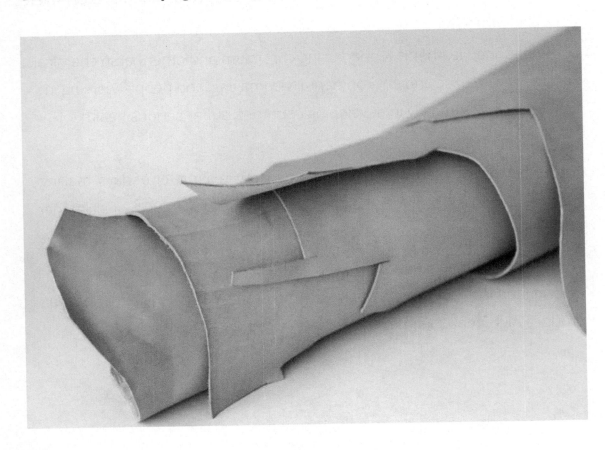

Different leathers for the various parts of the shoe

Upper Leather 1 to 1.5 mm (3 - 5 oz) thickness. Nearly all leather used for the uppers is cow or calf hides, and sometimes horse hides and kangaroo leather.

Calf hides are thinner and lighter than cowhides and make good shoe leather. Cowhides are often used for sturdier work boots. They could also be used for shoes depending on the look you want to achieve.

For the upper, it is best to choose leather from the shoulder, back or butt because the grain is tighter and has less stretch. Do not use the belly as an upper leather as it is too stretchy. However, belly leather is suitable to enforce the toe and heel areas, so a good option for the stiffeners and heel counters.

Top sole or insole leather, 1 - 3 mm (3 - 7 oz): I like using belly leather for the top sole as it is softer than the rest of the hide. You can also use the upper leather or any other veg-tan leather.

Midsole leather, 3 - 5 mm (7 - 12 oz), is a thick but soft leather sandwiched between the outer sole and the top sole. The midsole adds strength to the shoe and will stretch and mould to your unique feet for a custom fit with wear.

Lining leather, 0.6 - 1 mm (2 - 3 oz), is thin leather. I recommend calf or goatskin. If you get cold winters, you could line your boots with lambskin (look for second-hand coats), rabbit skin or woollen fabric.

Outsole leather 3 - 5 mm (7- 12 oz) is specially made for use as soles it is compressed leather much stiffer and sturdier than other types of leather. Some of the best veg-tan leather soles were made by the famous German tannery J.R. Rendenbach sadly they closed down in 2021. The latest news (2022) is that they have sold their recipe to the German Kilger tannery. They might start producing the legendary soles again at some point in the future.

The Tannery J & FJ Baker in England is another producer of quality soles. They cure the hides with oak bark for 8 to 14 months. The resulting leather soles are incredibly durable, hard-wearing, lightweight and water-resistant. Yes, they are more expensive than other leather soles, but they last 2 - 3 times longer than cheaper ones.

Sole leather is sold in sheets or already cut units. The sheets are more economical but if you just want to make one pair of shoes, you could get a sole unit.

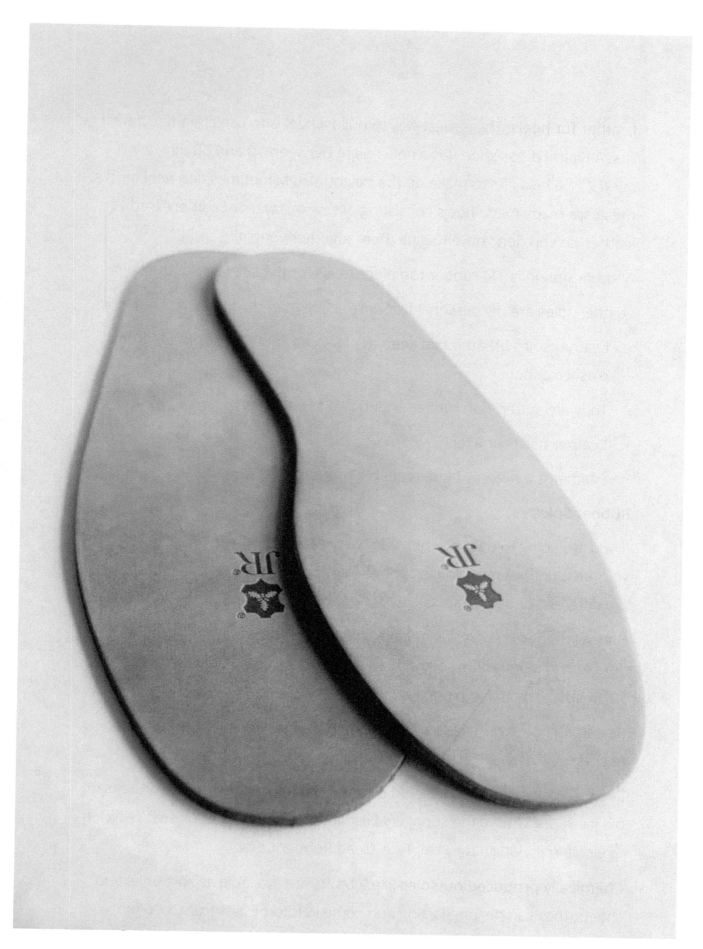

Leather for heels: The easiest way to build a heel is to use already-cut heel lifts. A typical dress shoe has a heel height between 10 and 30 mm. It will need 2 to 6 heel lifts to make up the height. You sometimes find heel blocks, these are ready made heels consisting of several layers of compressed leather, so you don't have to glue them together yourself.

Another option is 1/4 rubber top piece heels for the last layer of the heel.

Leather soles are my personal favourite soling material for several reasons:

- Leather soles breathe and keep the feet cool, unlike soles made from plastic/rubber
- They are softer than rubber and mould to your feet
- Leather has character
- Leather is a natural, biodegradable product

Rubber Soles

If you are going to use your boots in wet weather a lot, rubber soles might be your best option. You can get rubber soles as sheets or as sole units. There are different kinds available:

Natural rubber/crepe soles made from the sap of the Hevea tree. It is a flexible and long-lasting sole with an excellent grip on slippery surfaces and 100% sustainable and biodegradable.

Be careful not to purchase artificial crepe, which is cheaper but does not possess any of the features mentioned before.

Recycled soles, like bike tires, old rubber flooring, rescued conveyor belts or old car tyres. One of the suppliers I list at the back of the book sells recycled tyre sole rolls, which they call Tyre Tread Rubber Rolls.

Chemically produced outsoles like Vibram, are available as sole units and sheets, they can be long-lasting and come in thicknesses from 3 - 6 mm.

Heel lifts

Heel lifts 1/4 rubber top piece heel

Heel blocks

Recycled car tyre sole

Thread - I recommend using strong, waxed polyester thread, such as Ritza Tiger 1mm by German brand Julius Koch, designed for hand sewing. Natural threads made from linen or hemp do not last long on shoes before they disintegrate.

You can buy a roll of 500-metre thread, which will last a long time. Smaller amounts are available from sellers on Etsy or eBay. They are more expensive per meter, but you don't always want 500 metres of thread in one colour.

You will need about 30 meters of thread for one pair of boots. Probably a little less, just to ensure you don't run out while stitching.

Shoemaker's nails: To secure the sole to the last when lasting shoes. They are also needed to attach the sole and heels. You might need different lengths depending on the thickness of your soles and heels. For heel construction, serrated or buttress nails are best suited.

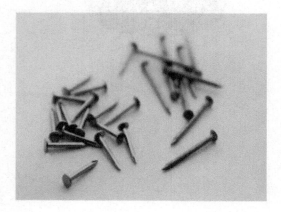

Clamps hold side seams and back straps together when stitching and soles and heels when attaching to the shoe uppers.

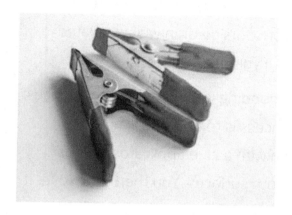

You could also use **double-sided tape** to hold leather pieces together when stitching side seams and back straps. **Masking tape** for pattern making.

Adhesives - My preferred adhesive is Renia Aquilim 315, a solvent-free, water-based adhesive. I use it for all bonding work in shoemaking, to bond leather with leather surfaces and rubber soles to leather midsoles.

The benefit of Aquilim 315 is its bonding strength to leather and rubber. Furthermore, it is a non-toxic and odourless adhesive, unlike neoprene cement which can cause health issues. Work outside or in well-ventilated spaces if you use it.

When bonding leather to leather surfaces, the process is to apply a thin film of Aquilim with a glue applicator or brush onto both surfaces. You then have to let it dry before pressing both surfaces together.

When bonding the lining to the upper, the recommended 30 minutes drying time is fine. When connecting the midsole to a leather outsole, I prefer to let the applied glue dry overnight. You can activate it with a heat gun (a few seconds) or a hair dryer in its highest setting. You can feel the activated glue; it is sticky to the touch.

When bonding rubber to a leather sole, I apply Aquilim to the rubber surface and let it dry for 3 days, then activate the glue with a heat gun. It seems like a long time to wait, but I prefer avoiding toxic cement. Details on working with Renia 315 are described in the chapter on attaching soles.

Tokonole gum to smoothen the flesh side of leather and burnish the edges of cut leather. A water-based, odour-free, non-toxic Japanese product, it binds leather fibre when applied with a burnishing tool.

Edge paint gives a finished look to the edges of leather projects. It is best applied with an edge tool or paddle. For the sole edges, I dye them with leather dye and polish them later with wax.

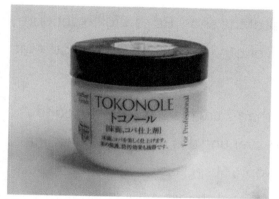

Tokonole

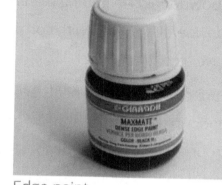

Edge paint

Yankee - Wax, an Edge Polish wax, creates a brilliant shine to the sole edge. It is applied with a hot edge iron. I use transparent and black.

Leather finish, I use a handmade 100% natural beeswax product (brand Bee Naturals), which enhances the natural beauty of leather and protects it from the elements.

Yankee wax

Beeswax

Leather conditioners such as Angelus Mink Oil, Neatsfoot Oil or Giardini Leather Conditioner.

Fiebing wax burnishing ink is available in neutral. Shades of brown and black are also available. I could not find it in the UK in smaller amounts, but in the US., you can find smaller bottles.

Talcum powder aids in getting the last out of the shoe. Be careful to get pure talcum powder, not mixed with cornstarch or other unhelpful ingredients that would have a contrary effect.

Shanks are optional if your heels are less than 2 cm high. They are used to add support in the waist of shoes/boots preventing this area from flattening to the ground with time. There are steel, wood, fibreglass and plastic shanks.I prefer wood shanks which can be glued on. Steal shanks would need extra metal fittings. Children's shoes do not require shanks.

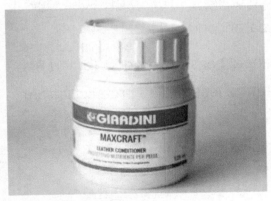

Leather conditioner

Wooden shanks

Eyelets for reinforcing punched holes and for decoration.

Boot hooks are useful for laces in long boots. They make getting in and out of the boots easier. You need a special setting kit for them.

Eyelets

Boot hooks

Hobnails, **segs** and **metal plates**. Hobnailing was a method of sole preservation in the 19th and 20th centuries. Hobnails can be applied all over or in areas of increased wear, such as the toes and heels.

Thin rubber soles can be glued to leather soles. This sole is available as a sheet or as half soles. After attaching them, cut off the excess with scissors.

Hobnails

Thin rubber soles

Leather Decorating Tools

Leather dye: I use water-based leather stains to dye leather. They are available in a wide range of colours.

Acrylic leather paint to draw onto the leather. It is best used to colour smaller areas but not for dyeing big leather pieces. Acrylic leather paint sits on top of the leather, whereas leather dye sinks into the leather.

Leather finishes can change the look of leather quite dramatically. I applied a gloss finisher to the red boots in this book.

A **Pyrography tool is** a heatable pen to burn drawings onto wood or leather.

Metal studs for that cool look.

Leather dye

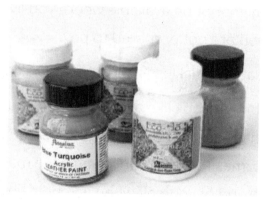

Acrylic paint

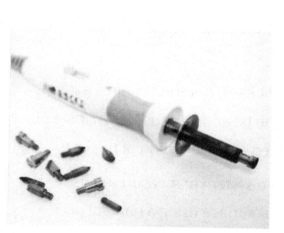

Pyrography tool

Decorative studs

Basic Techniques

Pattern Making

Why make our own patterns? Wouldn't it be great to just buy them like we buy sewing patterns or find them in books like this one? Probably a lot more people would try out shoemaking, but they might get frustrated once they realise that a ready-made pattern is unlikely to produce a good shoe.

A shoe pattern has to fit perfectly over the last you are using, and lasts, even of the same style, are all slightly different. So, if you purchased a shoe pattern, you would also have to buy the last used to make the pattern to create a shoe that fits snugly around it. That would limit your choice of lasts, and those lasts might not be available where you live, or they might sell out or have a price you are not prepared to pay.

Pattern-making is part of shoemaking.

It might look like a lengthy and complicated process, but if you follow the instructions in this book step by step, it is fun to see how the shoe pattern comes together. Once you have made it through the process, you will be so proud of yourself when you hold your first pattern in your hands.

In the coming chapters, I will describe the last taping method for creating patterns. It is relatively foolproof and used by most professional shoemakers of today.

Patterns can be designed directly on the last itself, but this requires a lot of experience, and I don't recommend it for the beginning shoemaker. Instead, we are designing the pattern on the flattened representation of the last.

I will describe how to make a pattern using a system of measurements to determine the layout of the pattern on a flat surface using a handful of reference points.

This method gives you a stronger sense of the metrics and rules involved with pattern creation, enabling you to create your own pattern variations.

Pattern Making Terms

Before we begin with pattern-making, let me introduce you to a few important terms that are universally used in the shoe pattern-making process.

Shoe Anatomy

Upper - the upper is everything except the sole

Upper and sole

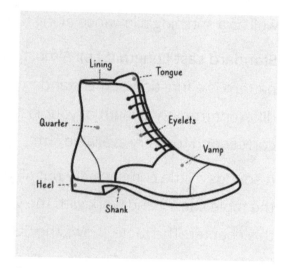

Sections of a shoe

Parts of a Last

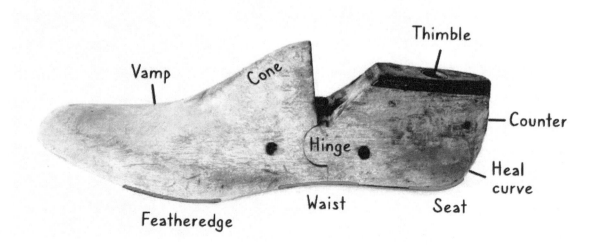

Design terms

Form - temporary 2D representations of the 3D last from which the patterns are created.

Mean Form - final 2D representation of the last from which the patterns will be cut.

Design Standard - a copy of the mean form with the design lines added as well as a stitching allowance along the bottom edge.

Standard Last Length (SLL): Almost every measurement used to create a pattern is a function of the Standard Last Length (SLL). The SLL is often slightly different from the length of your last. It is a standardised table of values that correspond to every available size.

It sounds a little complicated, but all you have to do is find your shoe size in the table shown and work with the value given in all calculations described on this chapter. The table shows the SLL of children to large adults in the UK and European sizes. I use European sizes throughout the book because that is what I am most familiar with. If you are in the US., please check out a size converter online.

| Size EU | 16 | 17 | 18 | 19 | 20 | 22 | 23 | 24 | 25 |
Size UK	0	1	2	3	4	5	6	7	8
SLL in inches	4	4 1/3	4 2/3	5	5 1/3	5 2/3	6	6 1/3	6 2/3
SLL in mm	101.6	110.1	118.5	127	135.5	143.9	152.5	160.9	169.3

| Size EU | 27 | 28 | 30 | 31 | 32 | 33 | 34 | 35 | 36 |
Size UK	9	10	11	12	13	14	15	16	17
SLL in inches	7	7 1/3	7 2/3	8	8 1/3	8 2/3	9	9 1/3	9 2/3
SLL in mm	177.8	186.3	194.7	203.2	211.7	220.1	228.6	237.1	245.5

| Size EU | 38 | 39 | 40 | 41 | 42 | 43 | 44 | 45 | 46 |
Size UK	5	6	7	8	9	10	11	11.5	12
SLL in inches	10	10 1/3	10 2/3	11	11 1/3	11 2/3	12	12 1/3	12 2/3
SLL in mm	254	262.5	270.9	279.4	287.9	296.3	304.8	313.3	321.8

Taping the last

The pattern-making process starts with taping the last and then marking specific points like the centre-line and vamp point. Next, we create the form and finally the design standard.

The first step is to tape the last to create a removable mould. Make sure to stick each strip of tape down along the whole length. To get an accurate result, avoid bridging it across the curves of the last. Ensure the tape conforms to the contours of the last and overlaps each strip halfway over the previous one.

In places, you will not be able to attach the tape exactly halfway on top of the previous layer because the curves of the last affect how it lies. This will not cause a problem as long as the strips overlap. Press each strip firmly to the last with your thumbs.

1. Stick a strip of masking tape up the centre front and back.

2. Starting on the inside, stick one strip of tape across the top, ending just across the centre front and centre back. Add another layer overlapping the previous strip halfway.

3. Continue adding layers all the way down the last until you reach the toe. Repeat this on the outside of the last.

4. Next, start from the toe by sticking a strip of tape straight across at right angles to the centre line. Continue adding strips overlapping halfway again until you reach the top of the cone.

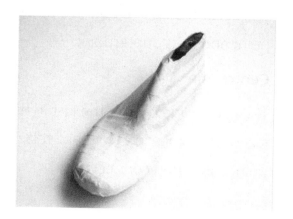

5. Starting from the top, add strips vertically down the outside of the last and work around to the inside until you meet the place on the cone, overlapping the first strips from the first layer.

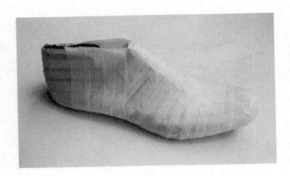 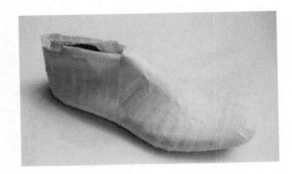

6. Trim the excess tape away from the featheredge of the last using a craft knife. The featheredge is the faint line that runs around the circumference at the bottom of the last.

Marking The Centre Line, Vamp Point and Counter Point

The second step in creating a pattern is marking the centre line, the vamp point and the counterpoint.

Centre line

The centre line divides the last in half lengthwise. It can be tricky to do this as it is not symmetrical. To make this process easier, mark a few easy-to-find points and then connect them.

1. Find the centre of the instep near the top of the last, which is roughly symmetrical and mark it **I** for "Instep".

2. Mark the centre front of the last at the very tip of the toe as **E**.

 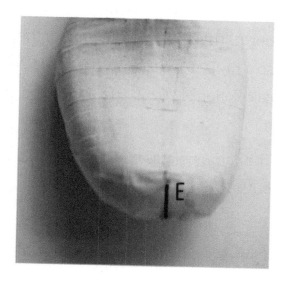

3. With a flexible ruler, draw a line down the front connecting the two points. If you don't have one, you could also take a length of tape, stick it to your cutting mat and draw a line down the middle. Place this lined tape down the centre of the last, aligning it with your marked points.

4. Do the same for the heel, which is more symmetrical and easy to eyeball.

 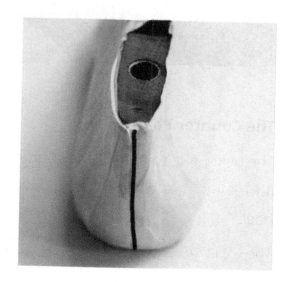

You should get these measurements as close as possible, but don't worry if they are not perfect. Any unevenness on either side will be averaged out in a later step.

The Vamp Point

Locating the vamp point (VP) is crucial in pattern making. It marks the widest point of the last and tells us where the facings should stop, and the vamp should begin. The vamp point is 7/10 of the length of the SLL, so if my last is a size 39, the SLL is 262.5 mm. My calculation is 262.2: 10 = 26.22 and 26.22 x 7 = 183.5 mm.

The vamp point is measured from the counter point (see next step) along the outside of the last to the centre line.

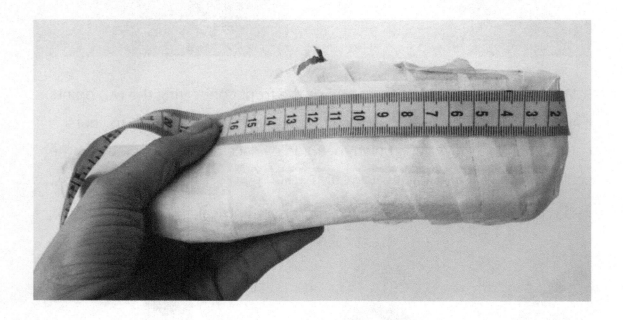

The Counter Point

The next point to mark is the counter point (CP). It indicates where the shoe sits on the heel.

The CP is 1/5 of the SLL measured up the back curve from the bottom of the last.

So my SLL is 262.5 mm : 5 = 52.5 mm.

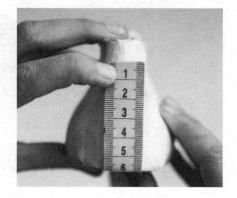

Creating The Forms

The steps below describe the process of creating the forms, which are 2D representations of the 3D last from which the patterns will be made.

1. Mark the inside of the last "inside form" and the outside "outside form", and add the number and/or name and size.

2. Using a craft knife, cut through all the layers of tape down the centre-front and centre-back lines to separate the inside and outside forms.

3. Carefully peel the inside section off the last, starting from the back-centre line to the front.

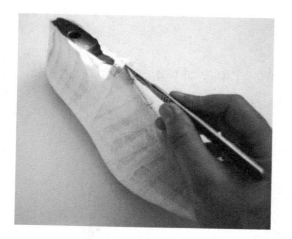 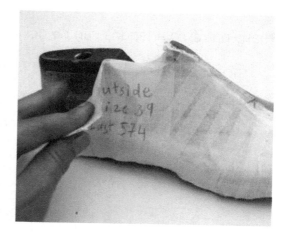

4. Make a few cuts along the toe line, a bit further down towards the vamp line and along the instep line. Tape the forms onto a sheet of thin cardboard on your cutting board, first pressing down the middle sections, then stroking towards the outside. Overlap the cuts to make the form lie flat.

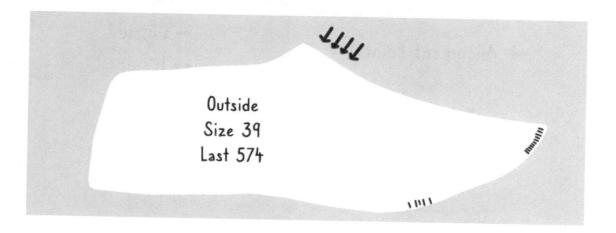

5. Repeat the process with the inside section.

6. Cut both forms out.

Creating The Mean Form

The mean form is created to remove any inaccuracies that might have occurred during the previous steps by averaging the difference between the inside and outside forms.

As the 2D representation of the last, it is the base of the design standard from which the patterns will be cut. Once you have created a mean form, many pattern variations can be developed.

1. Trace the outline of the outside form onto a piece of paper. Lay the inside form on top of this tracing and align it at the tip of the toe, the vamp point and the counterpoint at the heel. Trace around it.

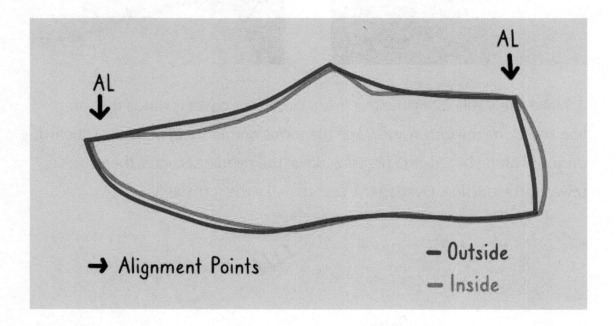

AL

AL

→ Alignment Points

— Outside

— Inside

2. Now find the average of these two shapes. Average the centre line by drawing a line that runs through the middle of the traced lines. Do the same at the heel and all the other lines that need averaging except the front bottom line.

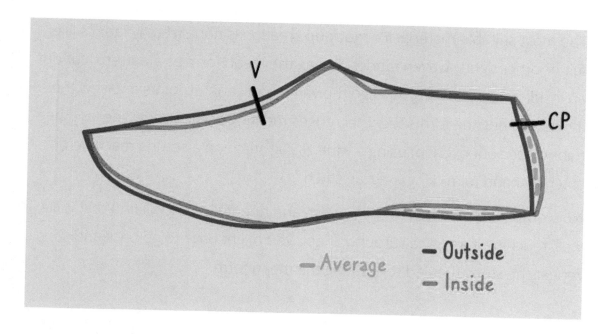

3. Cut through the new "average line" all the way around, except at the bottom of the front, where you should cut around the outside line. This is your mean form.

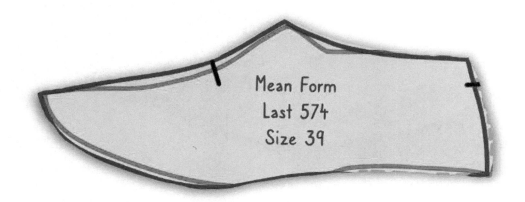

Mark the form "mean form", and add the last number and/or name and size.

Creating a mock-up

When you are a beginner with pattern making, it is best to create a mock-up of the mean form to get a feeling of how the pattern will fit on the last and check if it needs adjusting.

The most suitable material for mock-up creation is non-stretchy fabrics like felt or other tightly woven fabrics. Taking the mean form as a pattern, cut out an inside and outside form. Align the vamp and counterpoints and sew the inside and outside forms together, edges meeting at the centre line, and heel (fabric does not overlap) using a wide zigzag stitch on a sewing machine or stitch by hand mimicking a zigzag stitch.

Now drape the mock-up over your last, and hopefully, you will find that it fits well, touching it snugly all around. If not, you might have to go back and repeat the steps that led to creating the mean form.

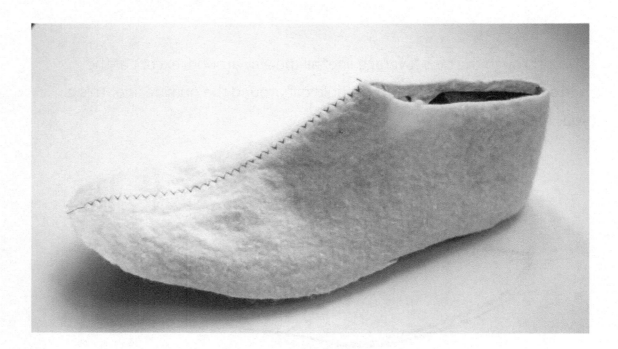

The final step in pattern making is to create the design standard which is a copy of the mean form with the design lines and stitching allowance added.

Please refer to the projects for learning how to make a design standard.

Creating A Sole Pattern

Before creating the sole pattern, pay attention to the bottom of the last, especially the inside feather edge. Lasts with metal plates like the ones shown below will have the feather edge already outlined.

If, on the other hand, your last is like the one shown in the second image, you will notice that the feather edge in the waist is not as sharply defined. You need to have a closer look to recognise the curve. You can draw along it, like I did on my last bottom, to outline the waist of your sole. Always follow the curve. A straight line in the waist would not make a flattering sole shape.

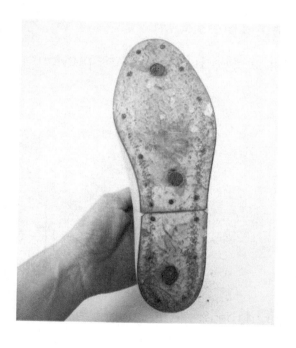 

Sole patterns are not design sensitive. The same sole pattern can be used for many different designs of shoes. All shoe designs in this book can be made using the same sole pattern.

1. Start by taping 2 strips of tape down the length of the sole.

2. Press each strip firmly to the last bottom and up the sides.

 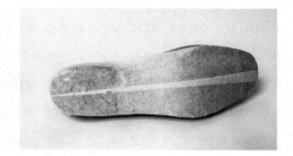

3. Add 2 strips at the front sides of the last and press down.

4. Add strips to the width of the last overlapping each strip with the previous one.

 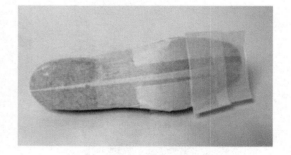

5. Continue in this way until you have covered the whole length of the last bottom.

6. Draw a line along the edge of the last with a pencil.

 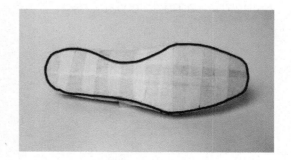

7. With a craft knife cut along the pencil line and peel off any excess tape.

8. Peel the sole pattern off the last.

 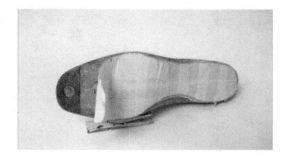

9. Tape the pattern onto a piece of thin cardboard and draw around the sole, this pattern will serve as an insole pattern.

Tape the pattern onto thin cardboard and with a compass add a seam allowance of 7 mm.

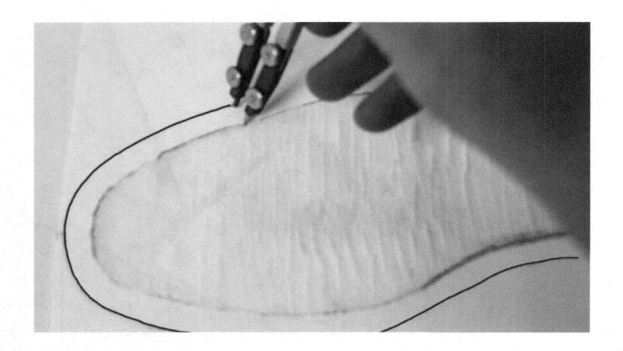

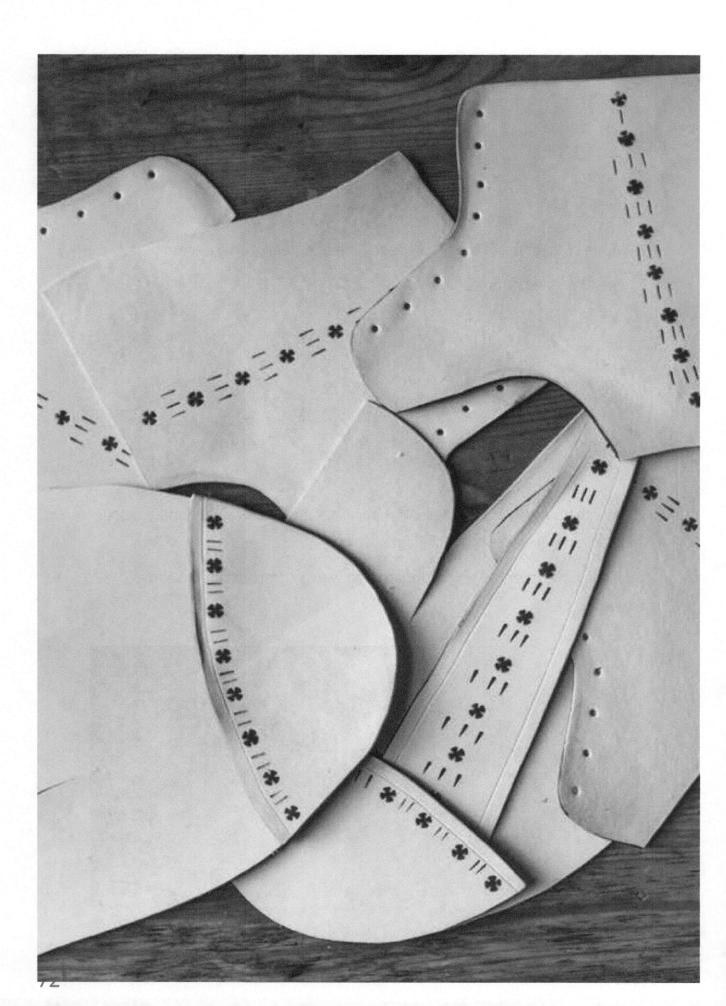

Cutting Out Leather

The grain of leather generally runs from head to tail but is not as precise as on fabric. If possible, try to lay out your pattern pieces with the grain roughly aligned along the lengthwise grain of the skin.

Always use the best parts of your skin for the most visible piece: the vamp. Lay out your skin face up, flat on a cutting table. Mark any holes or blemishes you wish to avoid with chalk. Never cut skins as a double layer.

Laying out your pattern pieces is similar to working on a puzzle. Start with the big pattern pieces and then fit the smaller pieces around the edges. Trace all the pattern pieces onto the flesh side of the leather with a silver pen.

Use leather shears to cut out the leather pieces. Always remember to flip over the pattern of your soles. You want a right and a left one. Also, check you have two pairs of quarters with a right and a left one. When trying to fit everything in, it is easy to forget, so before cutting into the leather, take a second to check you have all the pieces laid out correctly.

If the flesh side of your leather pieces is very fluffy, remove it by burnishing it with a glass slicker and Tokonole. You could also use a piece of fabric and some water. This will make skiving and adhering to the lining later on easier.

Cutting out the top and midsole

I cut the top sole pattern on the line but the midsole slightly outside. This way, I get a better edge.

With a bigger midsole, I can rasp and sand the midsole edge to fit the edge of the top sole and so avoid an uneven sole edge.

Cutting out the outsole

If you are using a sole unit, you don't have to cut out much depending on the size of these soles. You could trim them to about 2-3 mm excess around the shape of the sole. With a sole sheet, you could cut out straight lines and then cut out the shape, adding about 2-3 mm around it.

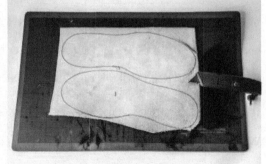

To cut the soles, place your sole sheet onto a self-healing mat and use a sharp knife. You could dampen the leather to make it softer and easier to cut.

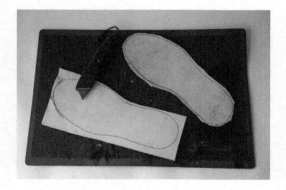

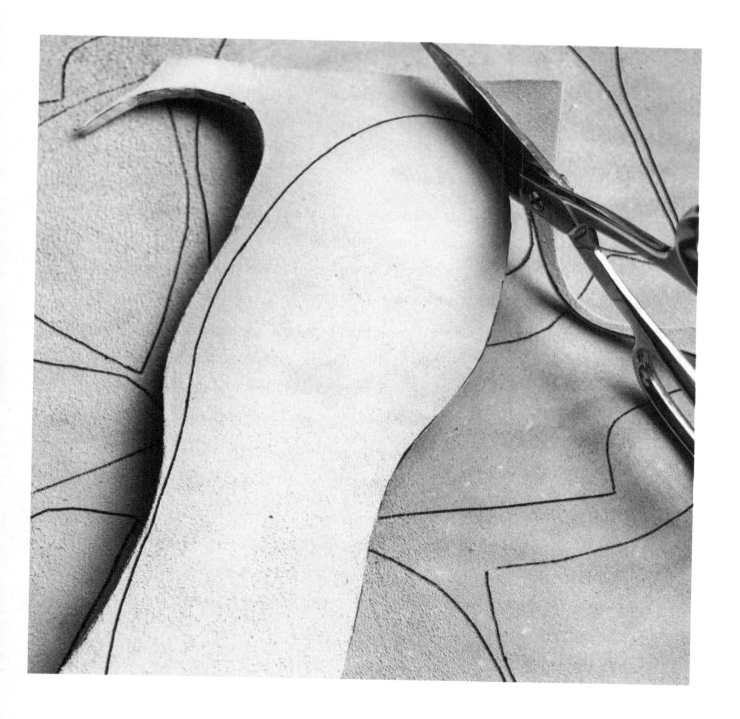

Dyeing Leather

Most industrial leather is dyed using chemical dyes in large drum vats, which give a very uniform albeit artificial look. Often you can not tell industrially processed leather from fake 'leather' anymore. In contrast, by dyeing veg-tan leather by hand each piece is unique. It gives the finished shoes an artisan look that makes them stand out.

I use water-based stains and rub them in carefully using cloths and lambs-wool. After dyeing, I allow the leather to dry for a day, then buff each piece by hand to achieve a nice sheen. I then apply a beeswax finish. Once the wax is fully absorbed, I polish the leather.

Treated this way, the leather will age beautifully and gracefully and develops a stunning patina naturally over time. Leather dyes are either alcohol or water-based. I prefer water-based dyes. They are easier to clean off equipment and are, in general, also more environmentally friendly.

In addition, water based-dyes do not dry out the leather-like alcohol dyes and have good colour bonding while maintaining the original softness of the leather. I use Giardini leather dyes (from Italy) and Identity water-based leather stains (UK). Fiebings also sells water-based leather dyes.

I recommend wearing rubber gloves during the staining process (I am not following my own advice here). You will also need lots of newspaper to protect your work surface.

Some dyes require a wool dauber, while others can be applied using sheep's wool, a sponge or a paintbrush. Always test the stains first on a piece of scrap leather. Usually, one coat of dye is not enough. Apply at least two and see if you like the result.

Skiving

To avoid bulk, some edges of the shoe pattern pieces are skived to create smoothly sloping edges. These are edges where two or more layers of leather overlap. These edges are thinned using either a skiving tool or a skiving knife.

The best surface for skiving is a solid and slick surface like granite or glass (like the glass slicker mentioned in the tool section).

A razor-sharp edge on your skiving tool or knife is crucial for skiving leather. Before starting to skive, dampen the leather slightly with a sponge. Put your pattern piece on a hard surface, flesh side up. Position the knife blade edge on the leather and shave thin layers off while keeping the blade at a low angle. Practise on pieces of scrap leather first.

Always skive on the flesh side.

If you use 1mm leather, you might not have to do much skiving. The photo below shows the areas that would need some skiving to avoid bulky edges and overlaps. More skiving has to be done when it comes to toe puffs and heel stiffeners which is explained in more detail in the next chapter.

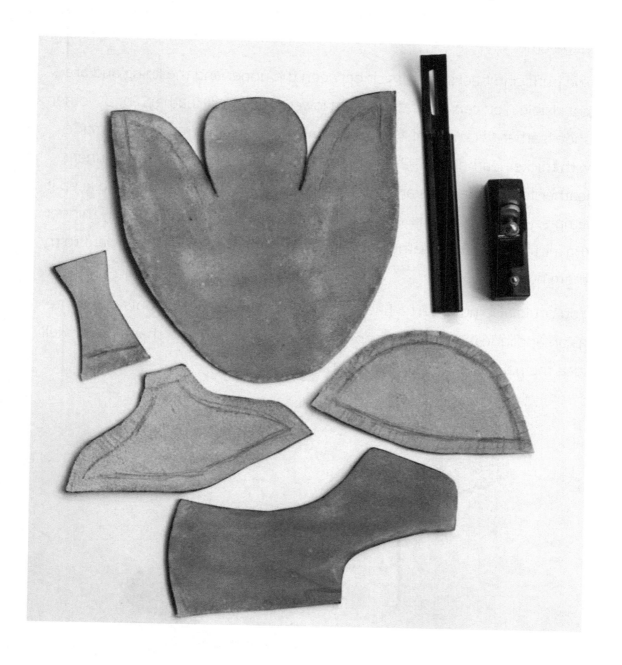

Making Toe Puffs and Heel Stiffeners

Toe puffs and heel stiffeners keep the shape of your shoes and protect your feet from forces outside the shoe. While most factory shoes are made with plastic stiffeners, it is possible to make them from veg-tan leather. Your shoes will be more comfortable with leather stiffeners than with any other synthetic stiffeners because leather becomes solid when dry but stays flexible at the same time.

Toe puffs and heel stiffeners sit between the upper and the lining and are not visible. You can make them from lower-grade belly leather. For a women's shoe leather thickness of 1.5 to 2.5 mm is enough. Men's shoes are made with thicker leather (2.5 - 3.5 mm). Shoemakers often use slightly thinner leather for the toe puffs and thicker leather for heel stiffeners, but to keep it simple, you could just skive the toe puff a bit more to make it slightly thinner. (Baker tannery offers leather pieces for both stiffener types if you want to try them out).

You could also not insert a heel stiffener and instead use an outside counter as an appliqué (overlay), and those two layers can hold the shape pretty well (see the painted boots in this book).

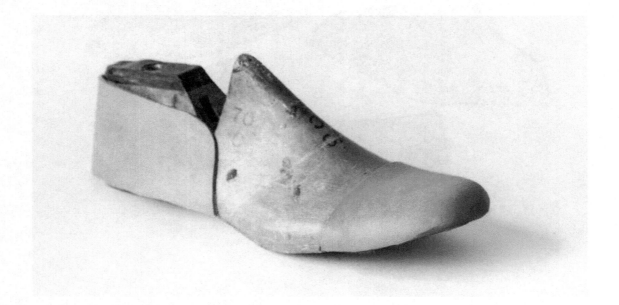

I would always insert toe puffs because you don't want that area of your shoes to collapse or stretch out after just a short time of wearing them. There is quite a lot of skiving involved in making the stiffeners to avoid bumps showing through the upper. All the edges are skived paper thin, so the thickness of the stiffeners tapers away gradually from the middle to the edges.

I use Renia 315 to glue the stiffeners to the uppers. Another product often used for this job is Hirschkleber (a German product). Both products dry rock hard and give strength and rigidity to the stiffeners. They can be revived with water if you want to repair or redo the toe area of your shoes.

If you live in countries where you don't have access to the products we have in Europe or the US, you need to be inventive. All sorts of alternatives are used: Wallpaper paste, flour mixed with water, and starch. In fact, Hirschkleber is made from potato starch with some preservatives added to the mix.

Toe puff

The skived end of the toe puff should be around 65mm back from the feather edge of the last at the toe. To make a toe puff pattern, get your vamp pattern and measure from the feather edge (not the seam allowance edge) 65mm. I put tracing paper on top of the vamp to draw it.

Cut it out and transfer it to thin cardboard.

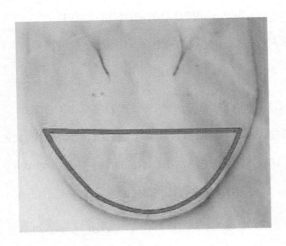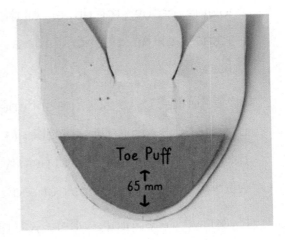

Heel stiffener

A heel stiffener sits at the rear of the shoe, creating a cup that secures the heel in the shoe and prevents movement within the heel. The length of the heel stiffener depends on the style of the shoe. Generally, it sits about 10mm behind the joint and 10 mm below the top line of the shoe.

Make the pattern the same way as the toe puff pattern, again using tracing paper to draw it and then transferring it to thin cardboard.

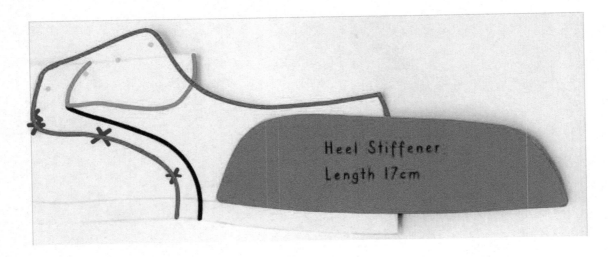

Preparing toe puff and heel stiffeners

1. Cut the toe puff and heel stiffener out of the leather.

2. Rough the grain side of the leather with a glass shard. This is to avoid the shoes becoming squeaky when walking in them (figure 1).

3. Skive the edges of the puffs and stiffeners on the flesh side. Aim for thinnish edges so there is a very smooth transition from puff/stiffener to the rest of the vamp once you adhered them to the vamp and quarters (figure 2 - 5).

Figure 1

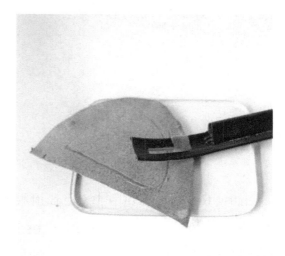

Figure 2

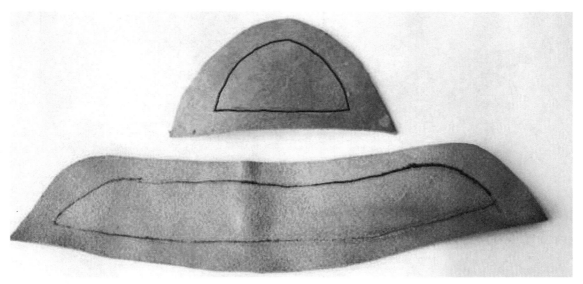

Figure 3

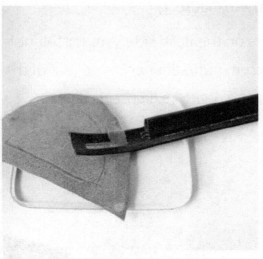

Figure 4

Figure 5

4. Using Renia 315 attach the puff to the vamp on the flesh side (figure 6 - 7). The grain side of the toe puff faces towards the last. Do the same with the heel stiffener (figure 8).

Figure 6

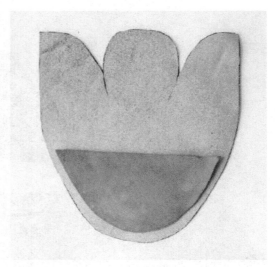

Figure 7

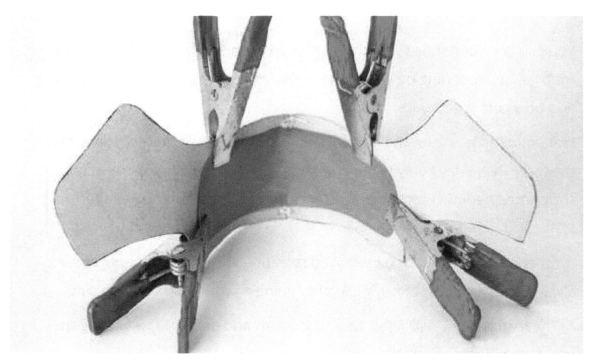

Figure 8

5. Glue the lining on sandwiching the stiffeners (figure 9).

Figure 9

Lining Your Shoes

You can line your shoes with thin calf or goat leather, woollen fabric, lamb or rabbit skin depending on what time of the year you want to wear your shoes and how cold it gets.

I recommend going for the natural lining as it comes into direct contact with the foot. These days only expensive shoes are lined with leather. Factory shoes are lined with cotton, polyester or canvas because it is cheaper than leather.

Synthetic lining can lead to increased sweating and unpleasant odours. As always, the extra cost of buying leather lining is worth it in the long run:

1. The leather lining will keep your foot warm and dry while regulating the moisture balance inside the shoe.

2. Quality shoe lining also makes your shoes last longer.

To make warm winter boots, I recommend sustainably sourced rabbit skin, which is warm and cosy without adding volume.

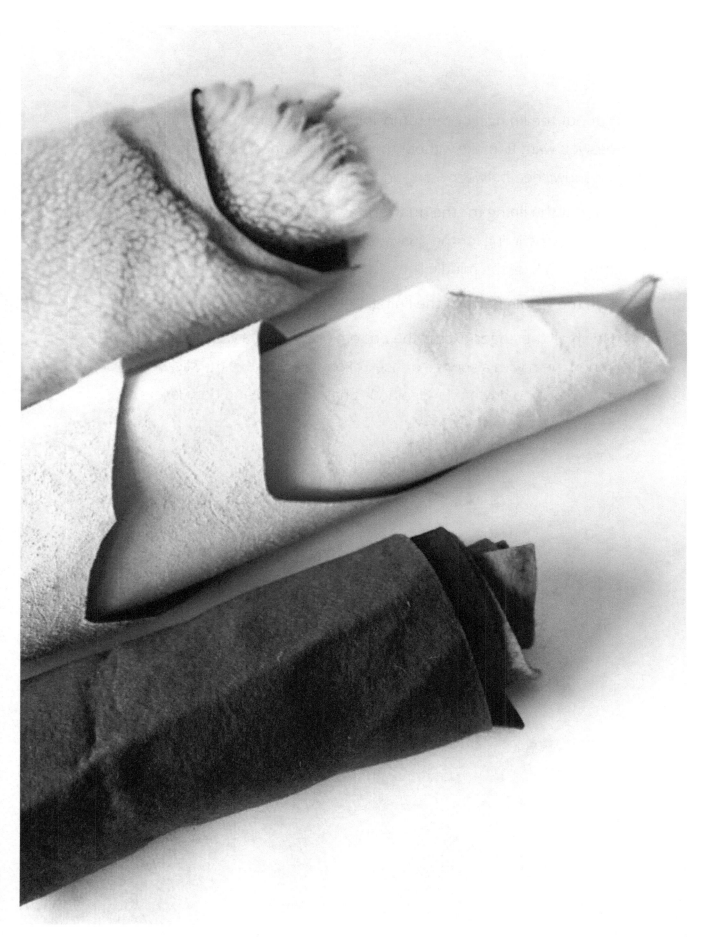

1. **Cut out the lining**: For the vamp lining use the same pattern as for the shoes you want to make without the seam allowance. Glue it on with the toe puff sandwiched between lining and leather upper.

2. **Cut out the lining for the quarters**, again without the bottom seam allowance. The lining for the quarters is cemented onto the sewn together quarters. To hide the middle line glue a strip of lining onto it.

3. **Dye the visible parts of the lining,** like the tongue and quarters .

4. **Finish all the edges** except the bottom ones using a wooden slicker. Dampen them with a sponge or use Tokonole and move the slicker with some pressure up and down the edge until it has softened and both layers of leather have merged.

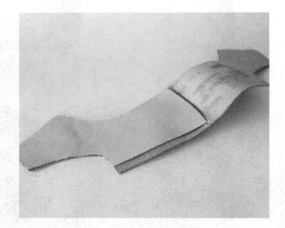
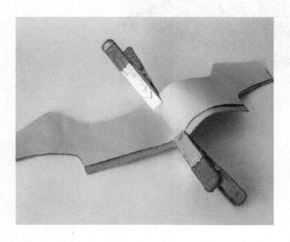

Setting Metal Eyelets

Eyelets are an optional step, personally, I like the look of metal on leather so I add them, especially on boots as there are lots of eyelets and they give the boots that something extra.

Metal eyelets come in lots of different finishes, silver, antique brass, gold, there are even coloured ones, so choose what looks good with the colour of your leather. You can buy eyelets that come with the anvil and driver, that way you are sure they will fit and set the eyelets properly.

I am using a flower punch here, eyelets are easy to set with it and hard-wearing. You only need the eyelets for this punch (no washers) and an anvil.

 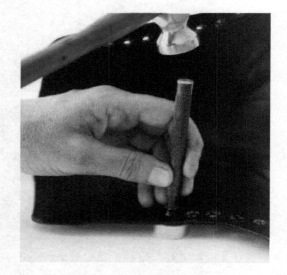

1. **Punch the eyelet holes** where you marked them, making sure they are big enough but not too big to hold the eyelets. They should fit tightly into the holes.

2. **Set the eyelets**: Sit the eyelet on the anvil. Put the driver or flower punch on top. Hit it with a hammer rotating it until the eyelet gets tight and set or the flower petals are spread out nicely.

Hand Stitching

There is a misconception that hand-sewn items are lower quality, weaker and less shapely than machine-sewn pieces. Nothing could be further from the truth! In fact, hand sewing has some distinct advantages over machine sewing.

First, aesthetically, stitches made by hand look more beautiful than machine stitching. Also, hand sewing allows for more exquisite details that set your work apart from the mass-produced stuff.

Secondly, technically, stitches made by hand are just as strong as machine stitches, provided you use the right thread. I have worn the same hand-stitched boots for many years without a single stitch breaking.

All you need is an awl, needle and thread, and you are in business! There is no need to buy an expensive leather sewing machine unless that is what you want.

Many shy away from hand sewing because it is slower than machine stitching, but in a busy and hectic world, sometimes it is nice to take a minute, slow down, and focus on what you are doing.

Another great benefit of hand sewing is that you can stop anytime and readjust if needed.

In this section, I describe the various steps involved in hand sewing: grooving, punching holes and the hand stitching techniques.

Grooving

Using the grooving tool drag a channel around the top sole, the vamp and quarters about 7 mm in from the edge.

This gives you a guideline along which you will sew and will make the stitching line look even. Also, setting stitches into a channel will protect the thread from wear and use.

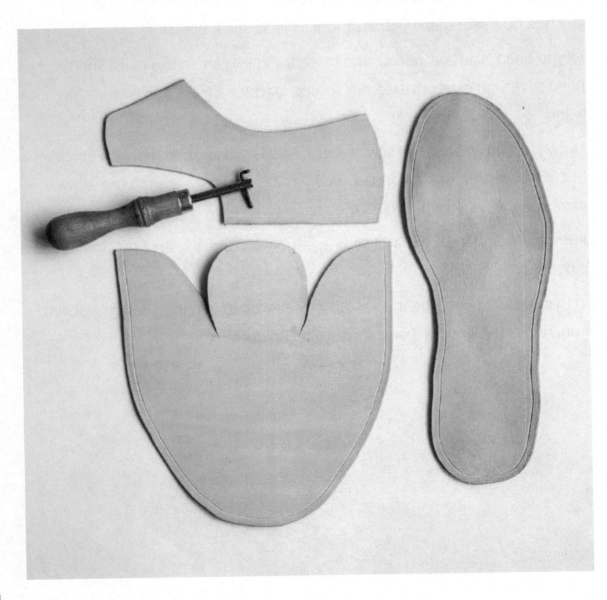

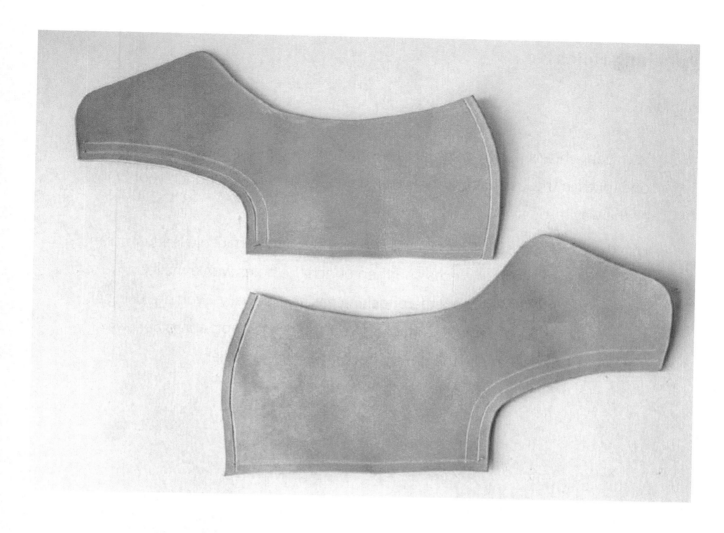

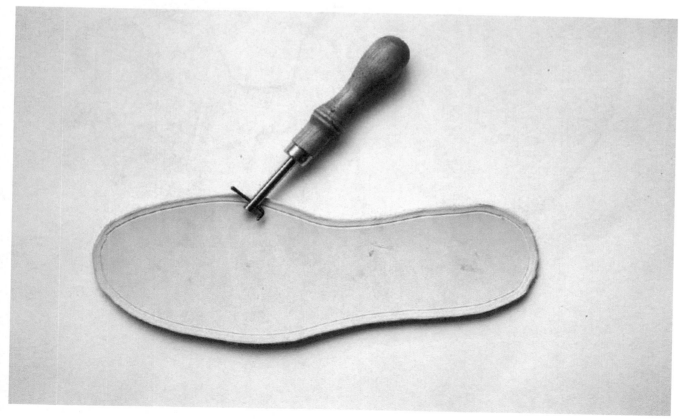

Punching Holes

With your chisels punch holes into the channels you just created. Always set one tooth in the last stitching hole made and make sure you punch your chisel all the way through the leather.

Use the 2 teeth chisel to get around curves. I put a thick midsole leather scrap piece under the pattern pieces and then punch the holes with a mallet. Wetting the leather will make the punching easier especially if you are using thicker leather for the soles (3mm plus). You could also apply some beeswax onto your chisels to make the pulling out of the leather easier.

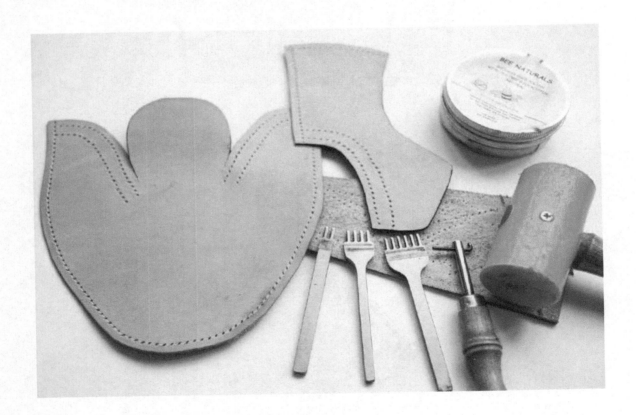

I punch the holes on the midsole with revolving punch pliers, I find this makes the stitching a bit more straight forward as the holes are bigger and easier to find when piercing into them through the top sole. Transfer the holes of the top sole to the midsole with an awl and then punch the holes with the smallest setting of the pliers.

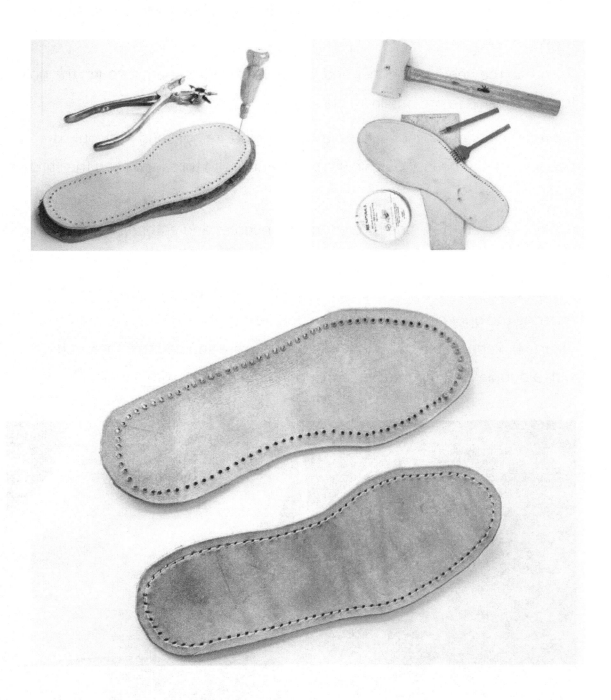

The X And Bar Stitch

The x and bar stitch is used to stitch together the 2 quarters edge to edge. You need 2 saddle stitching needles (or big-eyed needles) and thread.

1. With the edge groover, mark the stitching line about 3 mm from the edge. Punch slits with the chisels beginning and ending 3mm from the top and bottom edges.

2. Thread the needles at either end of the thread. Pass them through the holes from the inside to the outside (figure 1).

3. Pass the needles over each other to the opposite hole and back out. The needles are on the inside again (figure 2). Pull at the thread to keep the stitches snug.

4. Make an X on the inside by crossing the needles and entering the next pair of holes above (figure 3).

5. Now the needles are on the outside of the quarters again. Cross them entering the opposite hole to make a double bar of thread on the outside (figure 4). Repeat steps 3 - 5 until the quarters are stitched together, ending with a double knot (figures 5 and 6). Pound the stitches with a mallet.

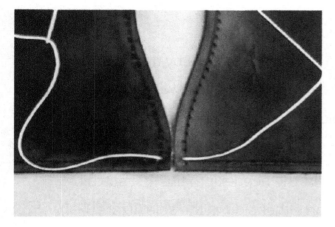

Figure 1

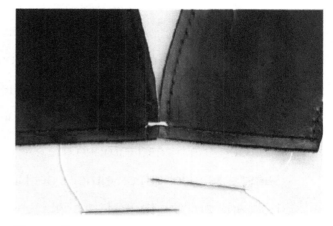

Figure 2

Figure 3

Figure 4

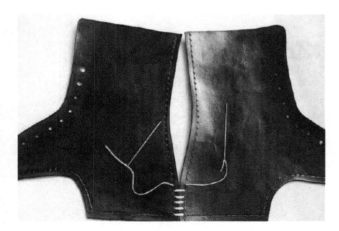

Figure 5

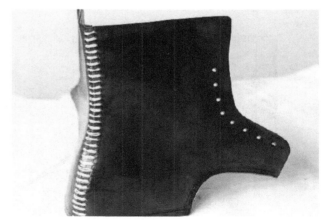

Figure 6

The Lockstitch

The lockstitch is used to stitch the upper to the sole. It is made by using a stitching awl. The lockstitch is the same stitch a sewing machine would make. One thread stays on the top side of the sole, the other one on the bottom.

1. Insert the thread through the eye of the stitching awl needle, keeping the same thread length on either side. Now, insert the needle into the first stitching hole and pull the thread through, leaving it on either side of the sole (figure 1+2).

2. Pull the stitching awl out of the first hole and insert it fully into the next hole. Now move the needle slightly down until a loop forms on the side facing the first stitch. If it forms on the other side, pull it to the side facing the first stitch (figure 3+4).

3. Pass the bottom thread through this loop and pull at each end. Make sure they lock within the stitching hole (figures 5 to 7).

4. Repeat steps 2 and 3 until you are back where you started. If you run short of thread repeat stitch in the hole where you need to stop, pull the thread out of the top side and cut it close to the leather. You can use the same method when finishing the stitching. Alternatively, you can pull the thread to the underside of the midsole and secure it with 2 or 3 knots.

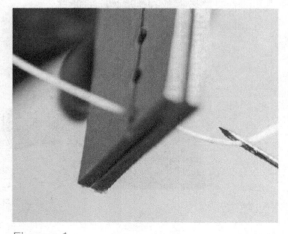

Figure 1

Figure 2

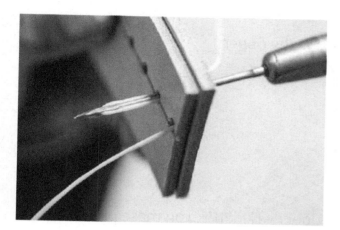

Figure 3

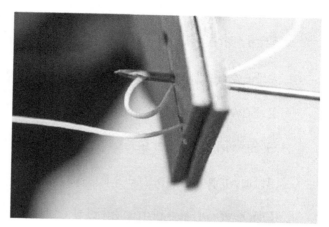

Figure 4

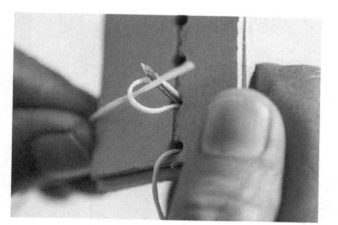

Figure 5

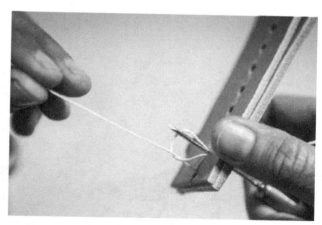

Figure 6

Figure 7

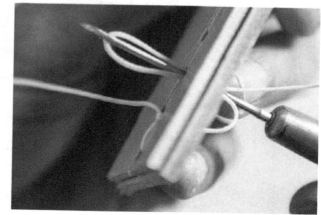

Figure 8

Constructing The Upper

There are several steps involved in constructing the upper:

1. Sewing the quarters together at the back.

2. Sewing on a back strap or heel counter.

3. Sewing on toecaps.

4. Sewing the quarters to the vamp.

Once you have completed these steps your upper will look like on these photos and your shoe/boot will be ready for lasting.

Building The Heel Section

There are a few possibilities for the construction of the heel section.

1. You could cover the stitching line of the quarters by stitching on a back strap. This construction would need a heel stiffener (figure 1+2).

2. You could sew the heel counter onto the quarters like an appliqué (figure 3+4). This construction does not need a heel stiffener.

For boots, you can combine the back strap with the heel counter when designing your back counter pattern, as I did with the painted boots in this book.

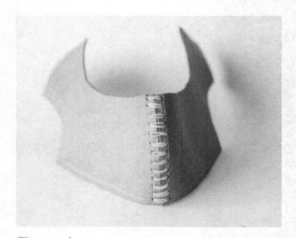

Figure 1

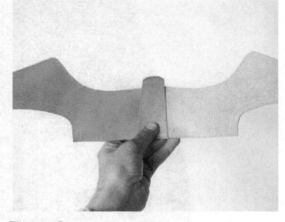

Figure 2

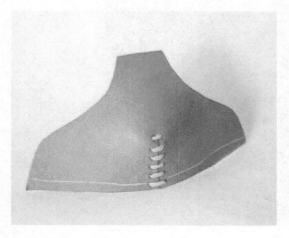

Figure 3

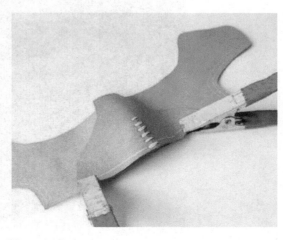

Figure 4

3. If you want to avoid the seam down the middle of the back counter, cut the counter out with a 20mm seam allowance. Fit it onto the sewn together quarters and trim along the edge of the quarters.

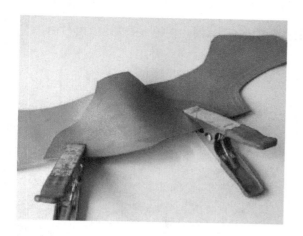
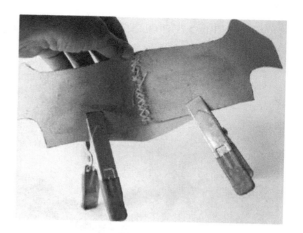

4. Another possibility is to stitch on the counter as part of the quarter. For this, you need to adjust your quarter pattern as shown below. This construction needs a heel stiffener.

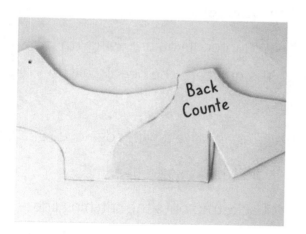
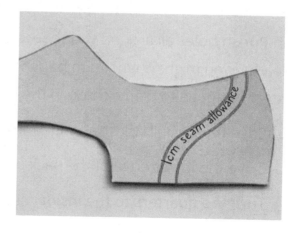

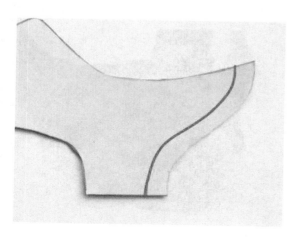
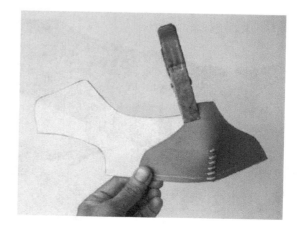

Another possibility is to stitch on the counter as part of the quarter. You would need to adjust your quarter pattern, as shown below. This construction needs a heel stiffener. Always skive the lower edge of the back counter and heel strap to avoid a bulky sole edge. If you are attaching the back counter as described in point 4, skive the quarter curves so they don't show through when lasting the shoe.

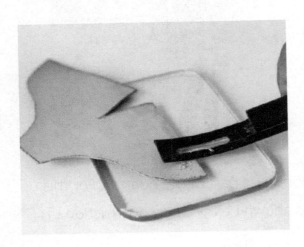 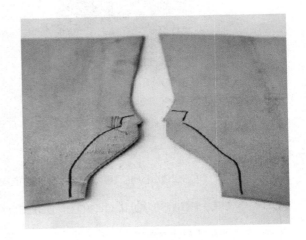

Sewing the Back strap / Counter Onto The Quarters

1. **Punch holes** all around your back strap/heel counter. If you are using 1mm leather you might not need to punch through the quarters, the needle will be strong enough to pierce through the leather.

2. **Edge finish** the back strap with a wooden slicker and dye it with edge dye.

3. **Skive the lower edge** of the back strap to avoid a bulky sole edge.

4. **Turn the quarters to the inside**, place your back strap onto the stitching line and hold it in place with either double-sided tape or clamps while you stitch it on.

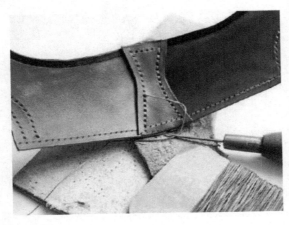 

You might want to stitch on pull tabs. Or you could cut the back strap about 5cm longer, fold it over and then secure it with a few stitches or a rivet.

This is what the before mentioned combined back counter and back strap appliqué on a boot looks like.

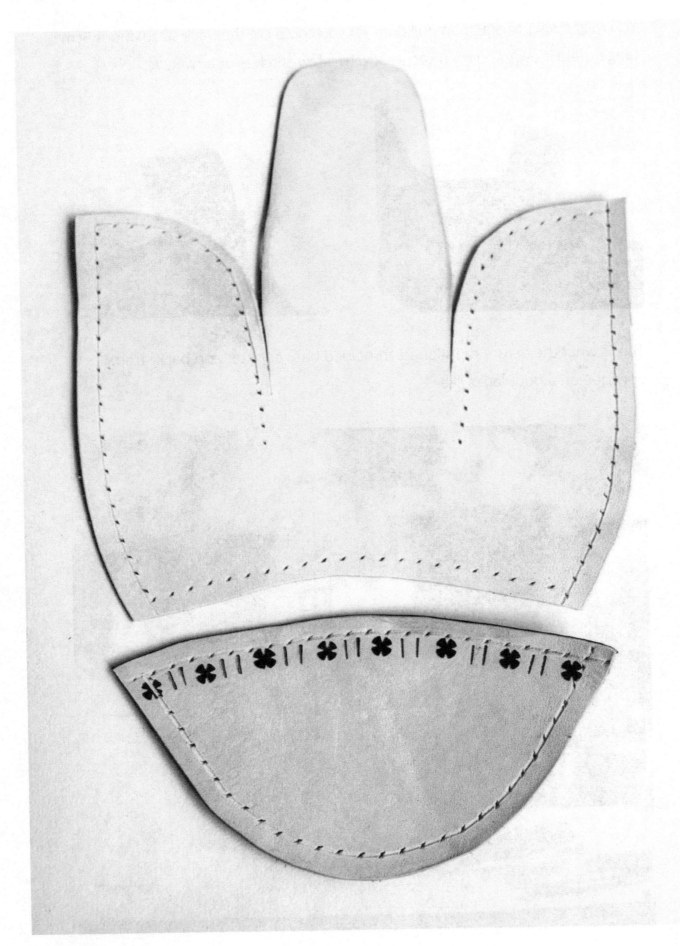

Adding A Toecap

A toecap adds interest to a shoe: you can dye them in a different colour from the rest of the vamp or decorate them like I did here with a pyrography tool or adorn them with studs.

Toecap Construction

1. Place the toecap pattern on top of the vamp pattern and draw in the top line.

2. Add a 10 mm underlay or seam allowance by placing the toecap edge about 10mm underneath the line you just drew.

3. Cut out your new vamp pattern.

4. Skive the edge of the vamp so it doesn't show through when lasting the shoe.

5. Stitch the toecap to the vamp using the lockstitch.

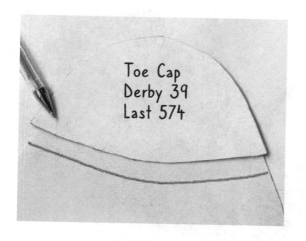
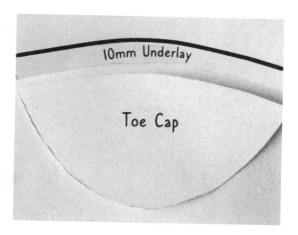
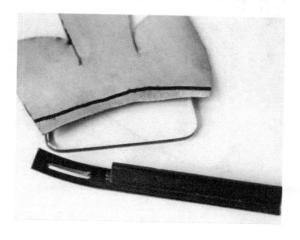

Sewing The Quarters To The Vamp

Placing the quarters in the exact right place is very important. When drawing the patterns you will mark the spots where the quarters have to be placed on the vamp. Consult the vamp pattern when positioning the quarters and make some piercings on the leather at the French curves' beginning, middle and end.

Hold the quarters in place with some needles, clamps or double-sided tape while you stitch. I usually start stitching at the top of the curve to secure it and prevent the quarter from sliding out of place.

There are a few options for how to stitch the quarters on. You could stitch them on with just one stitching line using the lockstitch. You could also sew a double line like I did on the red and black boots in this book. Another possibility is to use decorative stitching like I did on the brown boots.

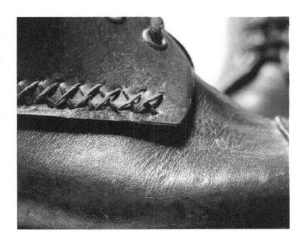

Lasting

The lasting process is where the shoe begins to take shape. The upper of the shoe is pulled over the last and drafted to it so it will set to its form and retain it when the last is removed.

Drafting means to mould the upper to the shape of the last by a series of strains or pulls along the hollows of the last. I soak the leather upper in warm water for 1 minute and then put it in a plastic bag for 30 minutes resulting in a soft and easy to mould material.

Sometimes I find it necessary to hold the leather down with a longish fabric scrap (only stiffer leathers need this treatment, in my experience). Once pulled down and stitched the vamp stays down and takes on the shape of the last. The shoe might sit a bit loose on it at first, but it will tighten while the leather dries. The patchiness will disappear too. I like giving the shoes another layer of dye after they have dried.

I usually leave the lasts in the shoes for at least 2 weeks while doing all the work on the edges and soles.

The following steps describe the lasting process.

Preparing The Soles

1. **Remove all fluff** from insoles and midsoles by burnishing the flesh side of the soles with a glass slicker or similar and Tokonole or water. With a glass shard or sandpaper, rough up the grain side of the midsole.

These measures are to prevent squeaky soles later when walking in them. The first shoes I made were very musical before I knew how to avoid them, so try not to miss this step.

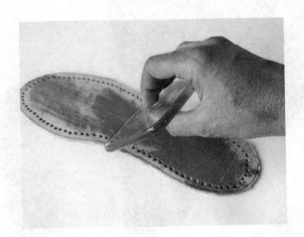 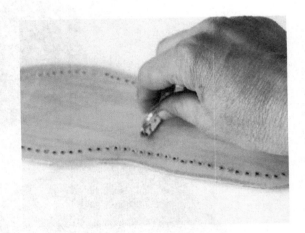

2. **Cement the top and midsole together**, the midsole with the rough side up. I try not to cover the holes with cement applying it on the outer edge and the inside surface. Make sure the holes line up on top of each other.

 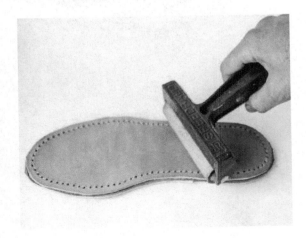

3. **Mark the points on the sole** where to hammer in the nails that hold the last and sole together while lasting and stitching the shoe. I use blue (or white) tack for this purpose which I press into the hole in the metal plate. I then press the last bottom onto the sole, and the blue tack will stick to it indicating where exactly to hammer the nails.

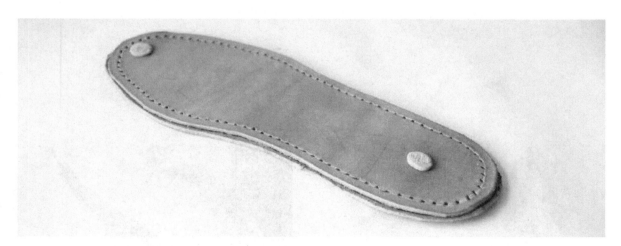

4. Prepare the holes for nailing by hammering the nails through the soles at the marked points.

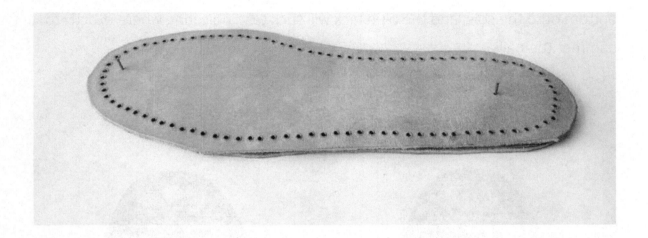

5. Attach the lasts to the soles. Make sure the last fits nicely into the punched line you created earlier. First punch in the heel nail and then the nail at the toe end. You could add a third one in the middle of the soles.

If all went well the construction will look like this.

Lasting The Shoe

1. Prepare the upper for the moulding process. First, soak the upper in lukewarm water for one minute, then put it in a closed plastic bag and allow it to sweat for 30 minutes.

Once ready for moulding, apply some talcum powder all over the inside surface of the upper. It will aid in getting the last out of the shoe later on. It can be messy, so you might want to grab a towel.

2. Shape the upper by pulling it over the last and massage it until it lays flat around the curves of the last. Use your lasting pliers to help you with this. They are designed to grip the leather and allow it to be pulled into shape. Check from all sides that the upper sits symmetrically on the last, especially the quarters from the front, right and left. They have to be perfectly aligned.

Fold up the stitching allowance all around the shoe. Weave sewing thread through the eyelets while stitching the uppers onto the soles.

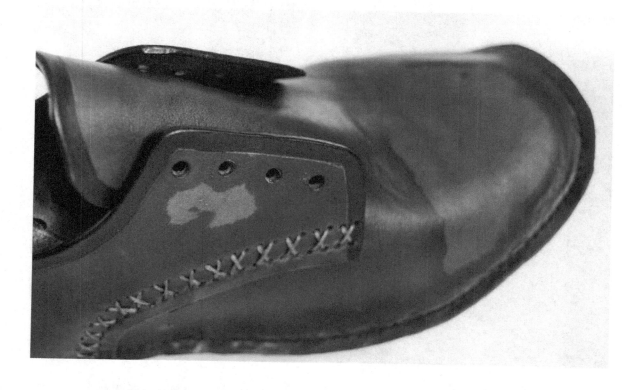

Stitching The Uppers To The Sole

Before you start sewing, make yourself finger gloves. You only need two for your index fingers. They will protect your fingers while stitching, and you can put more force into pulling the thread tight after each stitch made. You will need some soft, thin leather or other soft scrap leather. Measure around your finger and sew the leather together at the sides, it is simple, but I could not do without finger gloves.

After completing the lasting process, start stitching in the toe area. Continue checking that the upper looks good on the last. It sometimes happens that the upper is too far to one side, in which case it is best to undo the stitches and move it a stitch to the right or left.

I like stitching both sides at the same time. I make a few stitches on one side, then change to the other side and make a few stitches.

Attaching The Outsoles

Whether you use a rubber sole or a leather sole attaching the outsole is very similar. Shoemakers use sole presses to connect a sole firmly, but doing it by hand also works. I use Renia 315, a water-soluble glue that can be used for leather and rubber.

When using leather, you only have to wait 30 minutes (according to the instructions on the tub) to start working with it. In my experience, it is easier to attach the sole when you wait a day after applying the glue to the sole surfaces and then activate it with a heat gun or a hair dryer. It is so much stickier and really makes the job a lot easier.

When glueing on rubber soles, wait 3 days before activating the glue and cementing the soles. I also hammer in nails around the outsole and heel to prevent separation that might occur over time or in very wet conditions. Most lasts come with sole steel plates or at least a heel plate. Their purpose is that when striking the nails, they flatten and clinch to the insole to hold tight.

For the clinching, they have to make good contact with the steel plates, so they have to be the right length. Do not worry about this too much: adhesive and nails are usually enough. The clenching is an additional securing you might want to try one day.

You could attach shanks to the soles for additional support to the waist of the shoes. They are situated between the insole and outsole. Lower heels (2 cm and less) do not need shanks. I use wooden shanks to aid in preserving the form of the shoe over time.

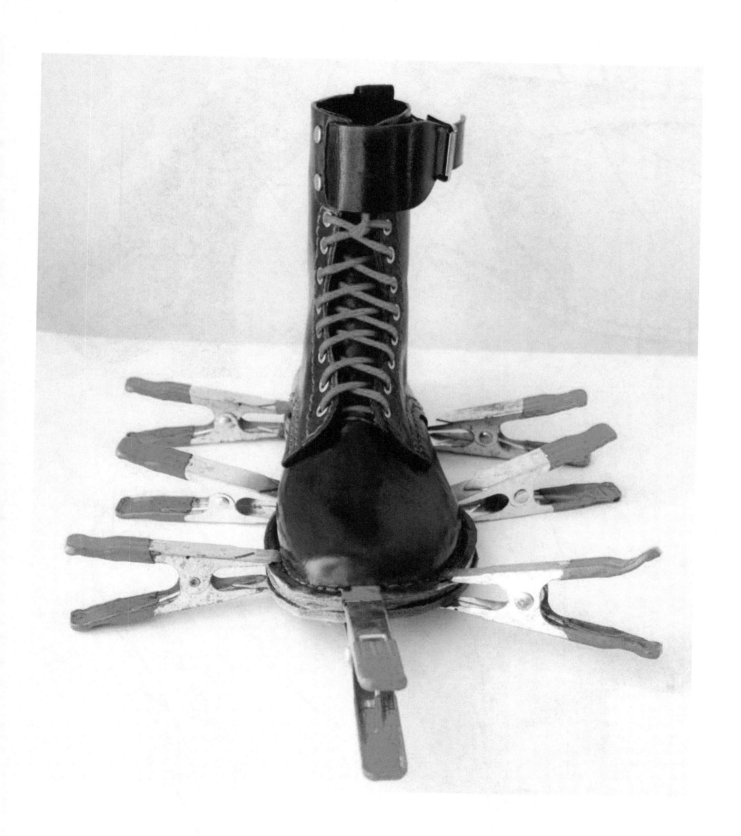

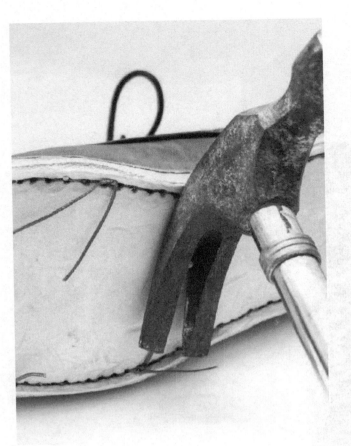

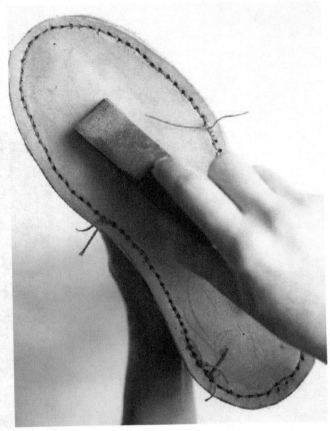

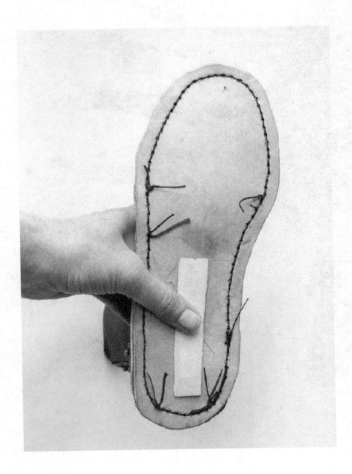

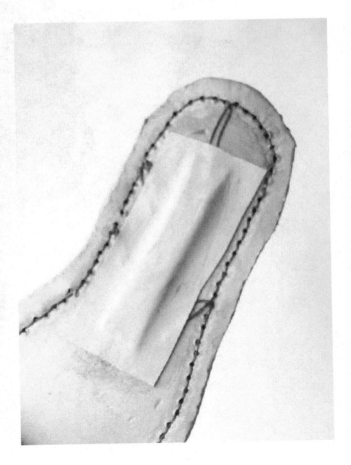

1. **Pull the nails out** using a tag puller or a similar tool.

2. **Rough up the surface** of the midsole leather with coarse sanding paper to allow the glue to penetrate the fibre structure.

3. **Glue on a shank** if you are using one. To prevent the shank from becoming loose over time, glue some lining leather on top of it.

4. **Apply Renia 315** to the midsole and outsole with a brush or glue applicator and allow to dry completely for a day (3 days for rubber), then heat activate the glue and stick the soles together.

5. **Hit the sole with a mallet**, first around the edge, then over the whole surface to pound out air. I also press a roller over the surface of the outsole. Hold the surfaces together with clamps and leave them to dry overnight.

6. **Cut off any excess soles** with a sharp knife. Hold your knife straight and cut in one go if possible.

7. **Hammer in nails all around the sole**. For precise placement of nails use a compass to space them. Pre-punching the nail holes with an awl will make the nailing easier.

Attaching Heels

The heel is built by stacking heel lifts together. I use only two heel lifts for my shoes and boots, which makes a heel height of about 15 mm. The heel layers are first glued together and then nailed together. I put 5 - 7 nails in each layer. For the first heel lift, I use sole tags.

For the outer heel layer, it is best to use serrated or buttress nails, which have circular ridges that act like teeth preventing them from pulling out. The length of the buttress nails is determined by the size of the heel:

• 5 mm thick heels or less use 11 mm nails

• 6.5 mm tick heels use 16 mm nails

• 10 mm or above thick heels use 20 mm nails

These nails go through the heel, outer sole and partway through the midsole.

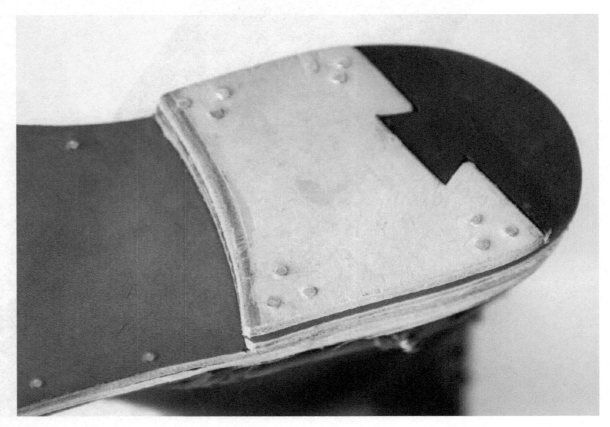

Try to nail each layer in a different pattern to reduce the chance of hitting a nail with another one. I like using 1/4 rubber top pieces for the last layer of the heel. But you could also use metal protectors or segs described in the next chapter avoiding rubber altogether.

Figure 1

Figure 2

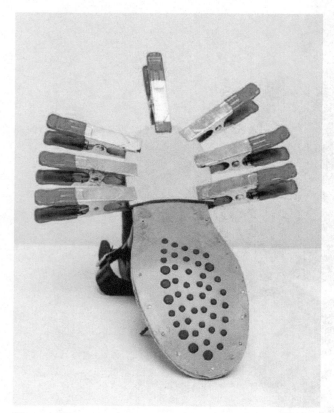

Figure 3

Figure 4

1. **Determine the positioning of your heel lifts**. Matching the side curve of the quarter with the front edge of the heel looks best, I find (figure 1).

2. **Sand the heel part of the sole,** then apply glue to the sole and heel lift (figure 2).

3. **Attach one heel lift**, pound the air out with a mallet and apply pressure with a roller all over the heel lift. Clamp the edges and let dry overnight (figure 3). The next day hammer in between 5 - 7 nails.

4. **Trim the excess leather off** the heel lift (figure 4).

5. **Glue on another heel lift**, repeating the procedure. Repeat this process until you have the heel height you want. If your second heel lift contains rubber, apply Renia 315 and let it dry for 3 days. Activate the glue as described earlier and stick the 1/4 rubber top piece on. Pound the air out and apply pressure all over the heel.

6. **Leave the glue to dry** for a couple of hours or overnight, then trim the excess leather off this heel lift. Straighten the corners of the heels with a sharp knife (figure 5).

7. **Hammer in a few buttress heel nails** all around the edge. You can pre-punch the holes with an awl for easier hammering and to avoid bending them.

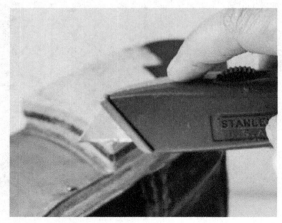

Figure 5

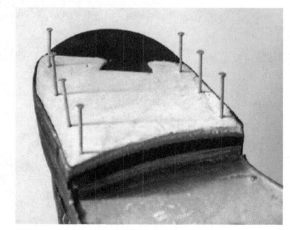

Figure 6

Protecting Leather Soles

I would like to introduce you to some ways to prolong the life of leather soles. This is an optional step: good-quality leather soles don't require add-ons. The metal add-ons I mention here are great if you want to avoid using plastic on your soles. They make a nearly 100% natural shoe (minus the thread). Available are old-fashioned hobnails, heel and toe plates, shoe protector segs and toe taps. All the metal protectors will make a click-clack sound when walking, so this might not be for everybody.

They are best attached by preparing the holes with a drill (smallest setting) or an awl and then hammered in. Alternatively, you could use a sole with a rubber inlay, like the ones I used on the red boots in this book, rubber segs or thin rubber soles that can be glued to leather soles.

If you get into rainy weather and your soles become saturated, change shoes as soon as possible, blotting away any excess water with a towel, and allow air drying. Once dry, treat your soles with a leather conditioner to keep them from cracking, peeling, and/or separating.

Heel and toe plates

Metal segs

The heel plate needs an extra little heel lift inside that you can cut out from a heel lift or a soling sheet.

The sole of this boot has metal segs,, you could also install rubber ones for soundless walking.

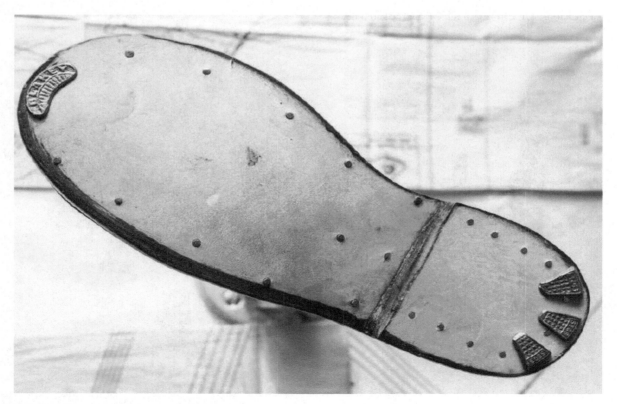

The easiest way to install hobnails and segs is to put the shoes/boots on the shoemaker's anvil with lasts still inside.

Another alternative is cementing a thin rubber sheet onto the front part of the sole as shown below.

Edge Finishing Soles

Finishing the edges of the sole is an essential step in the shoemaking process. It is to prevent the soles from getting ragged or frayed. You create a hard, shiny edge by sealing the fibres and fusing the different layers of leather. It will look more beautiful while protecting and strengthening the edge and making it water-resistant.

Finishing the edges of soles can take quite a bit of time. The good news is you will have great shiny edges by the end of it. I describe only the hand-finishing techniques here. Shoemakers also use sanding machines, the process is quicker, but they are not necessary to get nice edges.

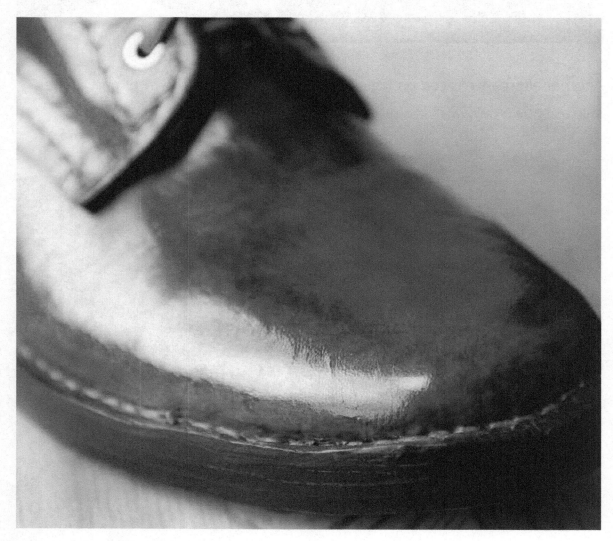

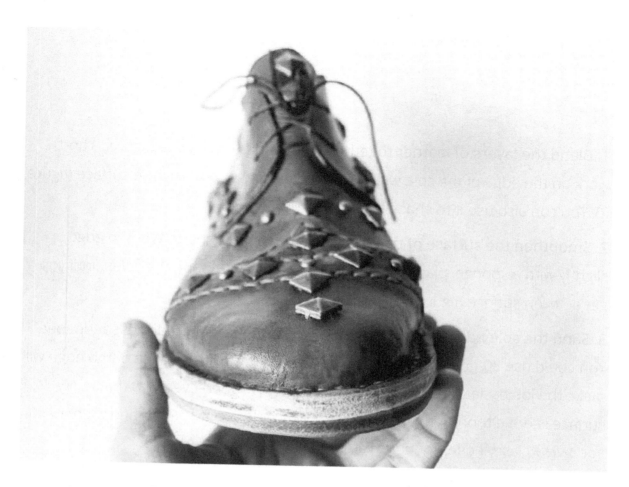

1. **Blend the layers of leather together**: Dampen the sole edge (figure 1) and work on the edge of the sole with a shoemaker's rasp to make one surface (figure 2). You can also use it to shape the heel (figure 3).

2. **Smoothen the surface of the sole edge** with a glass shard. Wet the edge slightly with a sponge, place the shoe on your lap and scrape the soles until you get an even surface (figure 4).

3. **Sand the sole edge** using a sanding block and different grades of sandpaper. You could use 80-grit aluminium oxide paper to start with. Again a damp edge will make the job easier (figure 5). Press hard and go around evenly so that every surface is done thoroughly. After the 80, you could use a 120 grit and then a 240. For a very glassy edge, continue with 400 and 800-grit sandpaper.

4. **Level and sand the inside edge of the heel** using the glass shard and sandpaper (figure 6).

5. **Bevel the sole edges**: With an edge beveler round off the edges of the soles and heels (figure 7).

Figure 1

Figure 2

Figure 3

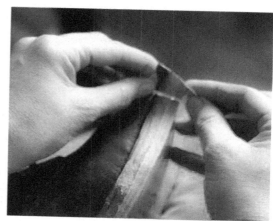

Figure 4

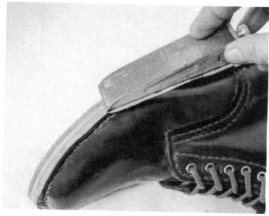

Figure 5

Figure 6

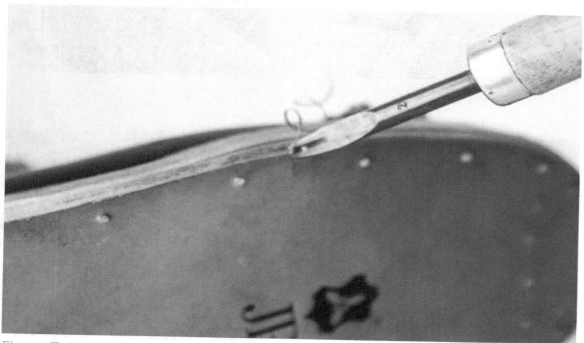

Figure 7

6. **Dye the edge** using a colour of your choice. I use water-based leather dyes and a paintbrush (figure 1). If you don't want dyed edges, you could just burnish them with the wooden slicker and some Tokonole (figure 2).

7. **Sealing and setting the edges**: Heat your edge iron over a flame and, once hot, dip it into the Yankee wax. Go along the sole edge with some pressure. This will cover any unevenness and tiny holes (figure 3). Burnish the wax into the edge with a piece of fabric for a shiny edge (figure 4).

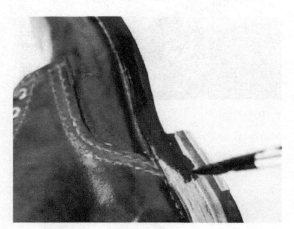

Figure 1

Figure 2

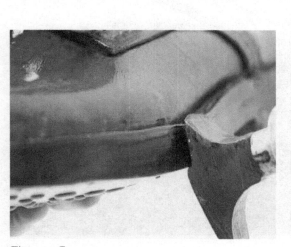

Figure 3

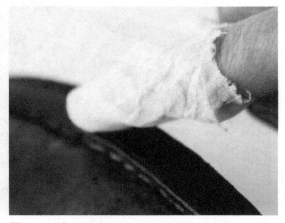

Figure 4

If for are not happy with your edges, you could pass by your local cobbler or shoe repair shop and ask them to go around the edges of your shoe with their sanding machine.

Another option is to invest in a tabletop sander. It does speed up the process. You have to make sure it is a type of sander that lets you get into the waist of a shoe. You do not need a sanding machine to get a nice sole edge. I just want you to know that this is also a possibility. There are advantages to hand-finishing the edges: you can get to all parts that a machine might not reach, and you have greater control during the process.

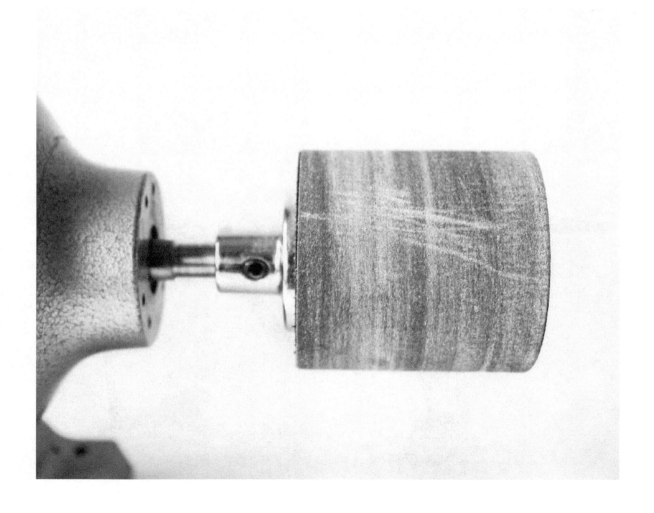

Cracking The Last

For best results, leave your shoes on that last for two weeks. One week is the minimum. Less than that will affect the quality of your shoes. They can stay on while you work on the sole and the edge finishing. Cracking the last is the last step in the shoemaking process. Lasts have to be broken at the hinge so you can get them out of the shoes without tearing up any seams.

For boots, use a lasting post as described in the tool section. For shoes, you could pull the lasts out using a metal pin.

Using a lasting post: First, open the laces of your shoes or boots. Then place the pin of the lasting pole inside the thimble of your last and slide the toe upwards or downwards to crack it, depending on the hinge type.

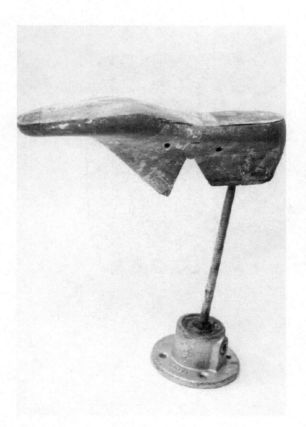 

Using a metal pin: Open the laces of your shoe and insert the pin into the thimble. A sharp tug towards you will cause the last to crack, and the shoe can be safely removed.

Caring For Your Shoes

After you have done all the hard work of making shoes or boots, you want them to last and look their best for a long time. Here are a few things you can do to prolong the life of your shoes and make them perform well from the beginning:

Wear them at home first. Break them in by wearing them around the house for a couple of days. This will soften up the construction and ensure a comfortable fit.

Grit your shoes. Try not to take your new shoes for a walk in the rain on day one. Wearing them in the dry enables a layer of grit to work its way into the leather soles, which acts as a protective shield for less favourable conditions. It also primes the soles with a layer of grip: new leather soles can be slippery in the wet.

Don't wear your shoes for two days in a row. Switch between your shoes daily to allow them to air dry.

Use wooden shoe trees. Shoe trees help air out your shoes during storage and keep your shoes in great shape while preventing cracking and wrinkling. Cedar wooden ones smell good, absorb moisture and refresh shoes. Insert them immediately after you have taken your shoes off when they are still warm. This will smoothen out any creases and retain their original shape.

Ideally, shoe trees are similar in form to the lasts the shoes were made over or even based on the original lasts. If you happen to you buy lasts from Springline (located in the UK), they sell corresponding shoe trees to their lasts.

Wet weather: Try to avoid wearing your leather-soled shoes in rainy weather. Leather is a porous material and will deteriorate in the wet. If you get caught in a shower, stuff them with newspaper or tissue paper and allow them to dry out naturally. Never dry wet shoes next to a radiator or another source of heat: the leather might crack.

Shoe horns are a great tool to preserve the back heel shape of your shoes and boots.

3. The Projects

The following projects include how to make

1. A Derby shoe and a variation of the pattern.

2. Ankle boots (up to 8 eyelets or up to 14 cm high).

3. Long boots (more than 8 eyelets or 14 cm plus).

4. Boots with a bellows tongue.

Throughout the projects, I will be referring to the basic techniques section

of the book in order not to duplicate instructions.

The Derby Shoe

For your first project, I recommend making Derby shoes. I show how to make a pair with no extras, so you can concentrate on learning the basics before becoming more adventurous. This pair of shoes has no toecap and just a back strap at the heel. In the following section, I will describe the process of making a Derby shoe, from drafting the pattern to constructing the shoe.

Step 1: Creating The Design Standard For A Derby Shoe

The design standard is a copy of the mean form with the design lines added as well as a stitching allowance along the bottom edge. It is used as the master from which all the pattern pieces are cut for an individual design. I am making a design standard for a size 39 (UK 6) Derby shoe with 4 pairs of eyelets. If you are designing for a different size, just put in your own numbers when doing the calculations.

1.Follow all the steps in the pattern-making chapter starting on page 56 that describe the **creation of a mean form**.

2. **Draw around your mean form** onto a thin card.

3. **Mark the CounterPoint (CP)**: Mark the corner of seat **S** and measure 53 mm upwards. This is your **CP**. This is a calculation we made earlier (SLL: 5 = CP). Now measure up 1 cm and mark the back height **B**.

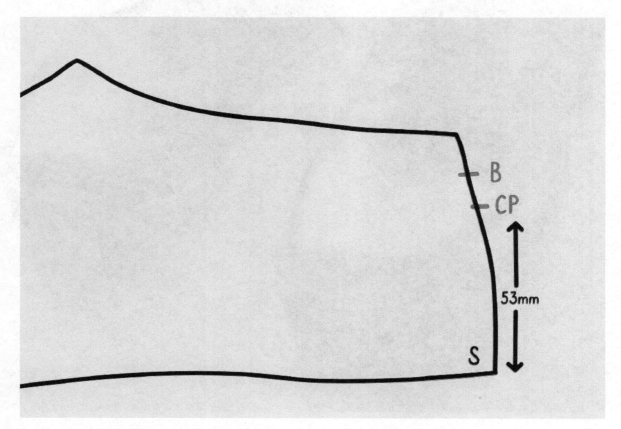

4. Mark the side height (A). This is to make the quarters of the finished shoes fit comfortably underneath the ankle bone. Divide your SLL by 4 and mark point **D** (1/4 of SLL), measuring from **S** along the bottom line.

Now divide your SLL by 5 and mark point **A** (1/5 of SLL) by measuring from point **D** at 90 degrees to the bottom edge.

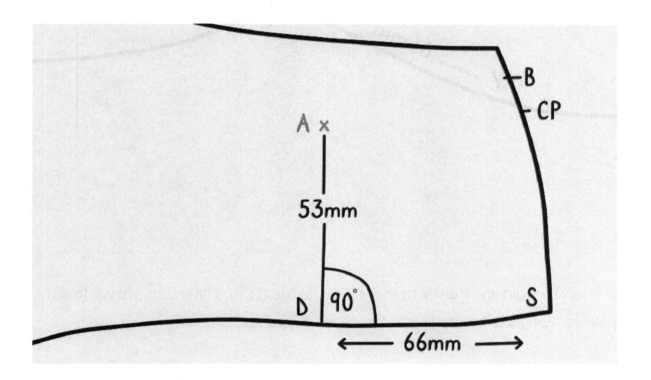

5. Mark the vamp point (V), you already calculated it on page 64.

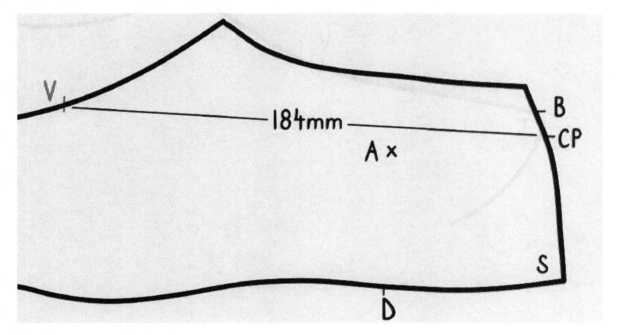

6. Determine the instep point I: SLL: 4 (1/4 of SLL).

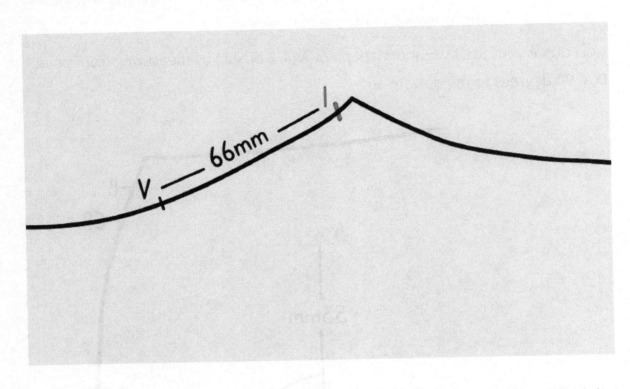

7. Draw the fold line from **V** to the top of the toe (**T**). At a later step we will fold the pattern along this centre line to create the full vamp.

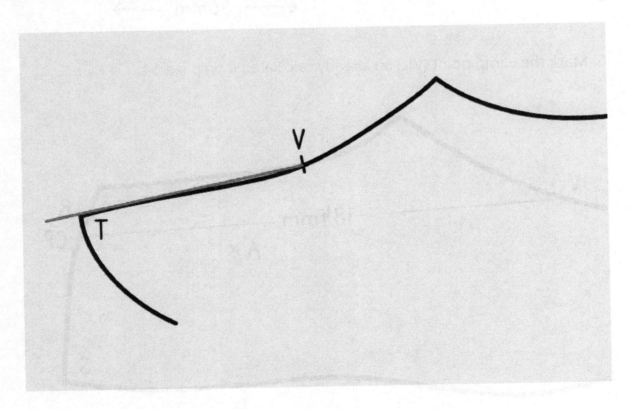

8. Draw a line from **V** to **X** which is 90 degrees to the fold line and mark point **F** which is in the middle of this line.

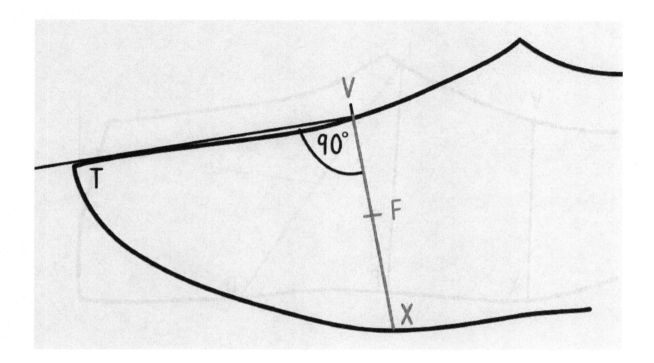

9. Draw a parallel line to **VX** starting at **I** to **P**. Mark point **C** which is 1/4 of the distance along the line from **P**.

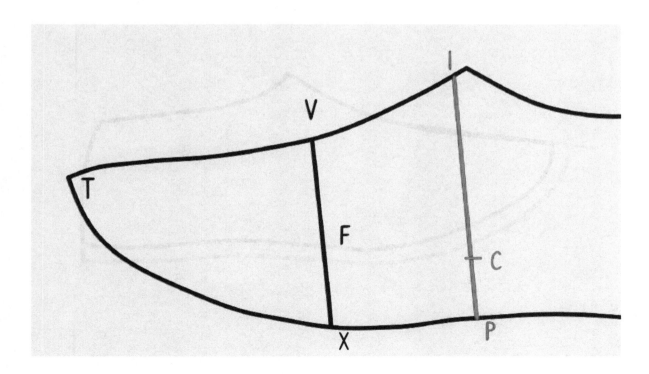

10. Draw a line from **I** to **D**. Draw a line from **B** through **A** meeting line **ID**.

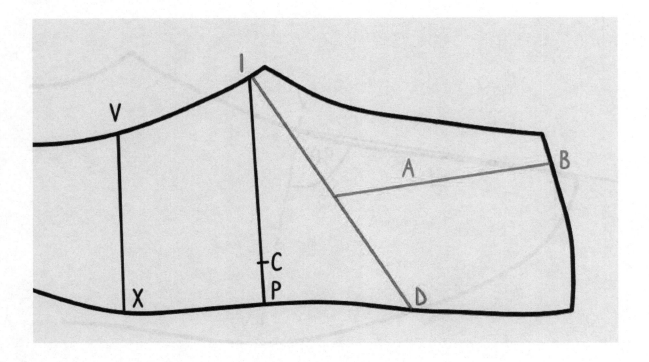

11. With a wing compass add 7 mm stitching allowance.

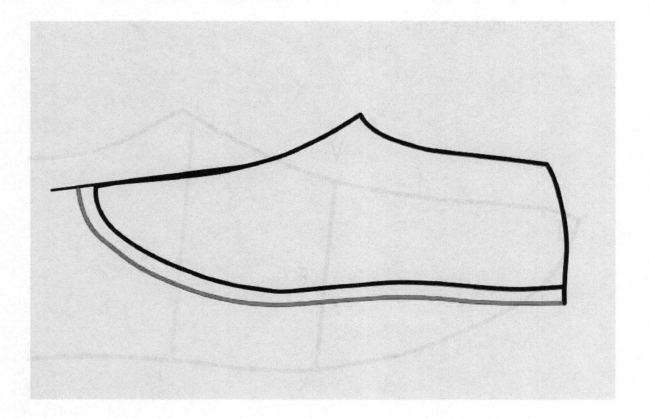

12. Draw a curved line from **F** through point **C** to just beyond **P**. You can eyeball this or use a French curve ruler or a professional footwear pattern ruler.

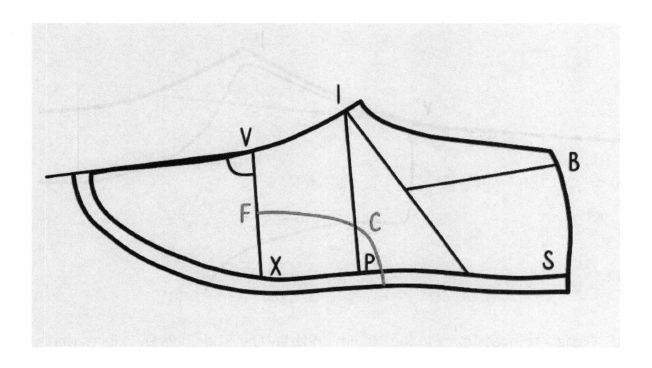

13. Draw the top-line curve starting from **B** through **A** passing near **I**, slightly underneath the top-line (about 3 mm) to V and down to **F**. Round the corners off.

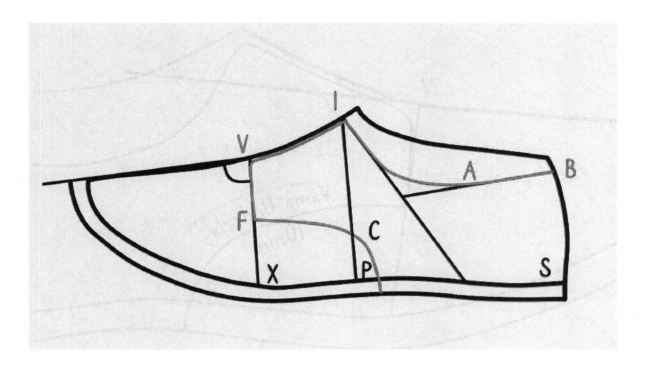

14. Extend the crease line to beyond the quarter line and mark point **R** which is 25 mm along this line from **V**.

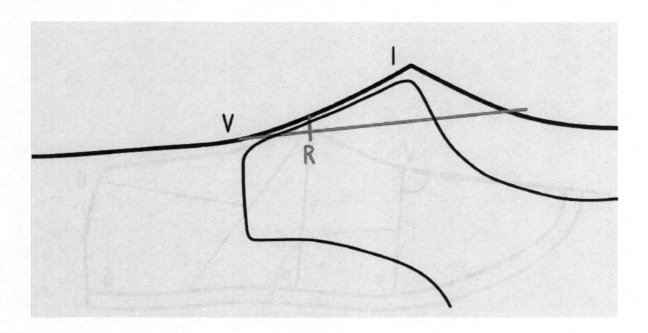

15. Using a compass mark in the 10 mm underlay line. The underlay is increased to 12 mm in the throat to ensure that the opening won't be visible when wearing the shoes. The line curves upwards and meets point **R** on the fold line.

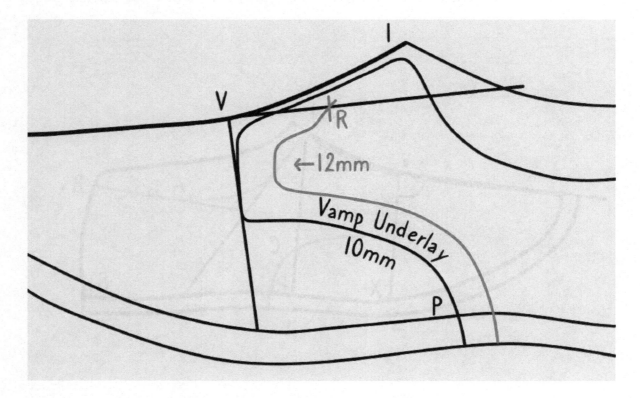

16. Mark point H, 10 mm from the edge of the quarter. Draw in the tongue shape, 90 degrees to the fold line at H. At its widest point, the tongue measures 32 mm.

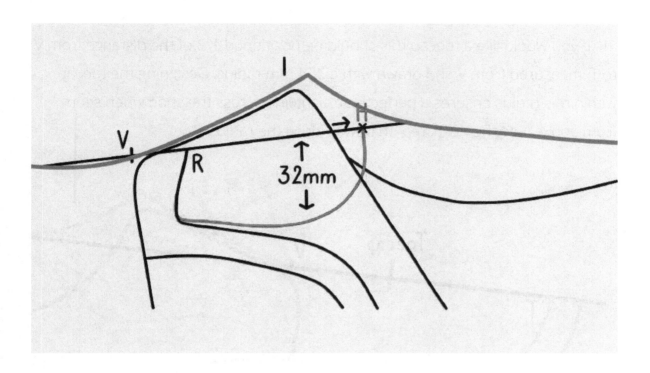

17. Mark in the four eyelet positions, they are 10 mm in from the edge of the facing. Rub out the construction lines.

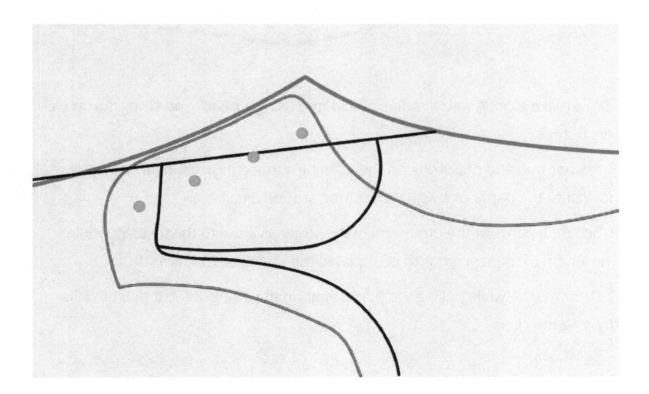

18. If you would like a toecap this should be positioned 1/3 of the distance from V to T, measured from V and drawn with a 254 mm radius. Designing the toecap within this radius ensures a perfectly straight line across the shoe when seen from above. See the next step on how to draw the radius.

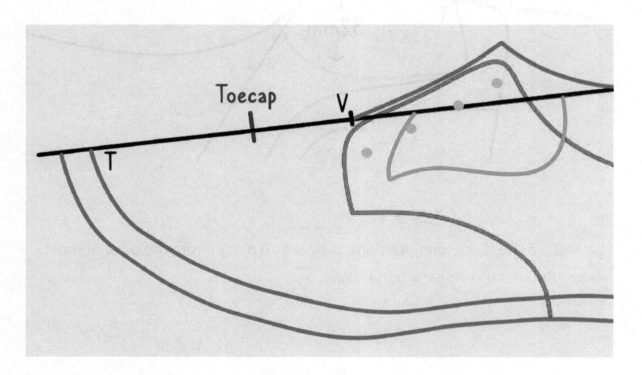

19. To make a circle with a radius of 254 mm using a pencil and string, follow these steps:

1. Anchor one end of a string on the drawing surface by pressing a pen point down into the paper or by tying the string around a nail.

2. Secure a pencil at the other end of the string as close to the tip as possible. The length of the string has to be equal to the radius of 254 mm.

3. Draw a circle while pulling the pencil tight on the string. Keep it taught while drawing the circle.

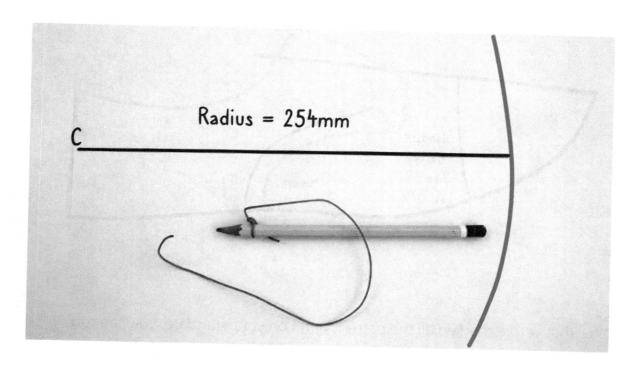

20. Cut out your design and place it in the circle, the centre point of the radius is on the fold line as shown on the photo then sketch in the toecap line.

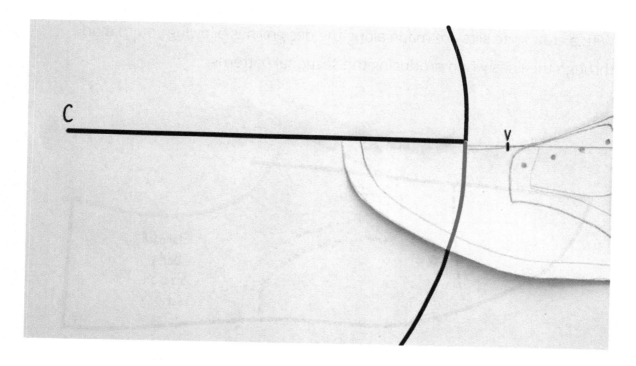

21. Note on your design standard which style it is, size and last number.

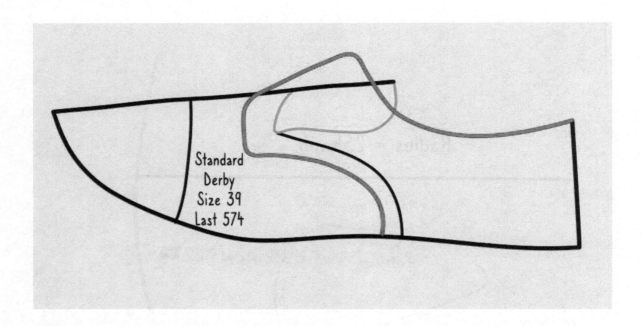

Now that you've marked all the pattern parts on your standard, you can turn them into individual pattern pieces.

Step 2: Cutting sectional patterns

With a craft knife slits are made along the design lines allowing you to mark through the lines when producing the sectional patterns.

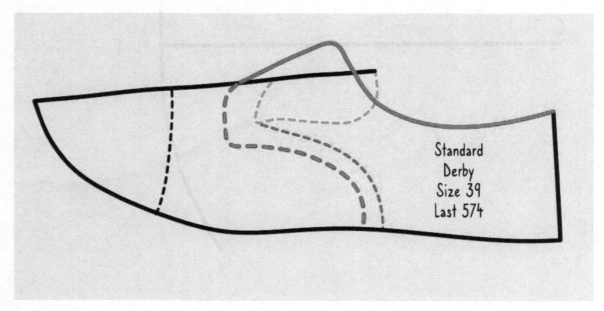

Vamp

1. Fold a piece of paper and position the standard along the fold line. Draw around the stitching allowance edge from the toe to the vamp underlay line.

2. Mark through the vamp underlay line from **R** to the edge of the stitching allowance.

3. Pierce through the quarter shape at each point shown with a green cross using a nail or other sharp tool.

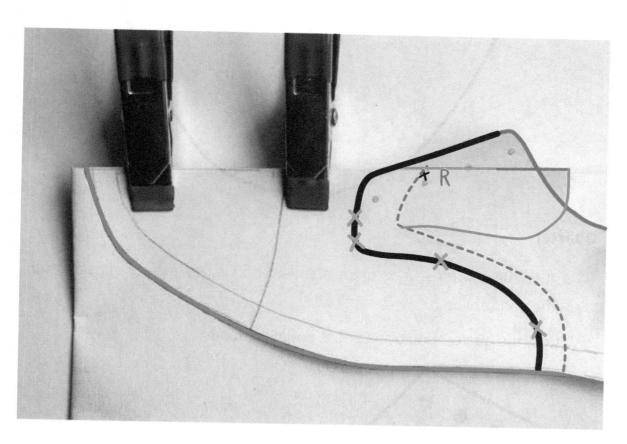

4. Cut out the vamp section from the folded paper and mark the piercings with a pencil.

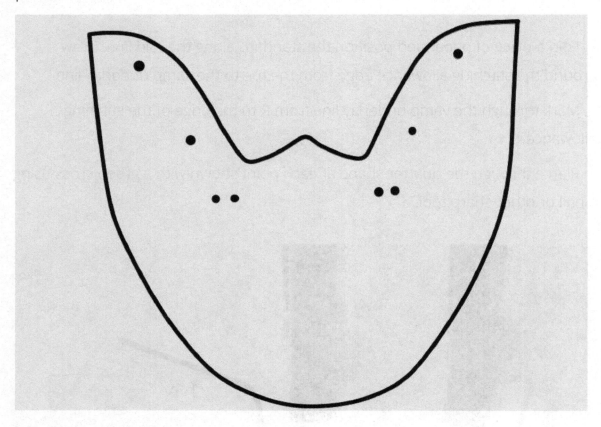

Quarter

1. Position the quarter section of the standard onto a single piece of paper and mark the quarter lines.

2. Cut out the quarter and transfer the eyelet positions.

Quarter
Derby
Size 39
Last 574

3. To get a better-shaped back curve, draw a 90 mm radius for a lady's shoe (115 mm for a men's shoe and 100 mm for children's shoes) and draw a line from the centre to the edge of the circle. Place your quarter inside the circle, and the centre of the heel meets the centre line.

Sketch in the back line as shown in the photo.

Cut out your new back line.

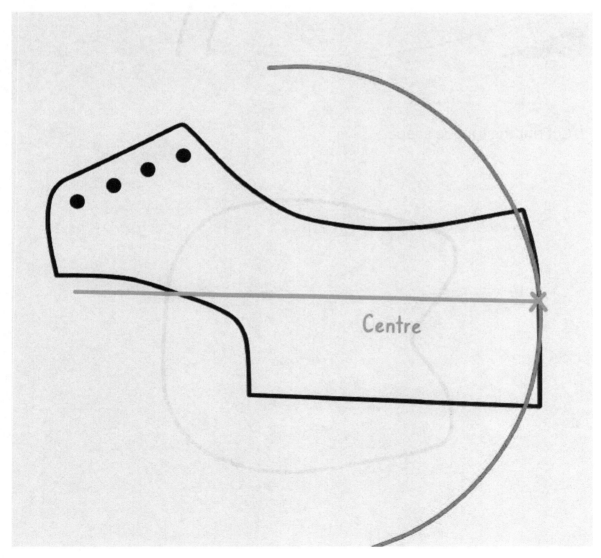

Tongue

1. Position the crease line of the standard on a folded piece of paper. Mark through the tongue shape and the vamp throat line.

2. Cut out the tongue shape.

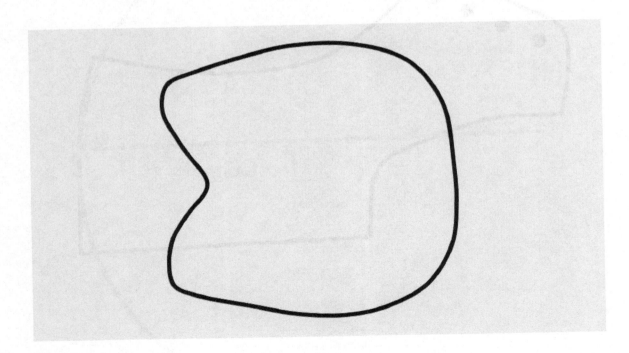

3. Position the tongue inside your vamp and secure it with tape. Now draw around the vamp and cut out your new vamp plus tongue shape.

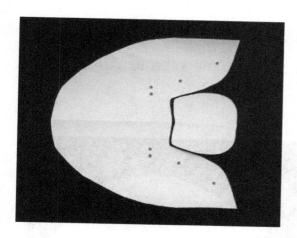
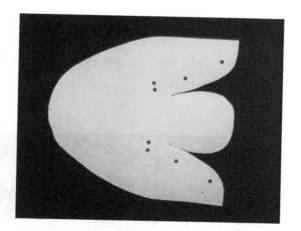

4. Create the inside of the vamp pattern: Position your Mean Form along the crease line and transfer point **J** onto the vamp pattern. Next, draw the inside line (blue line on the Mean Form) onto the vamp pattern and cut along it.

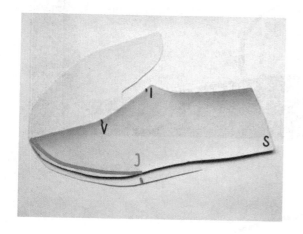
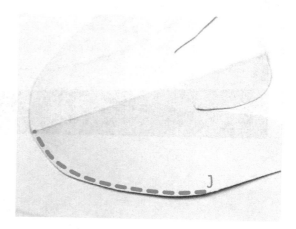

Mark the inside of the pattern.

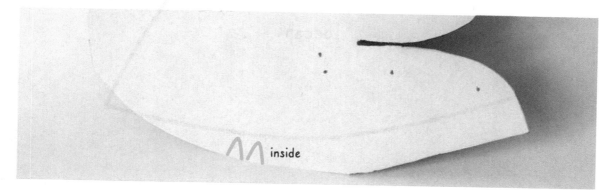

Toecap

Place the design standard on a piece of folded paper, upper edge aligned with the fold line. Draw around the lower edge and mark through the design line. Cut out the toecap.

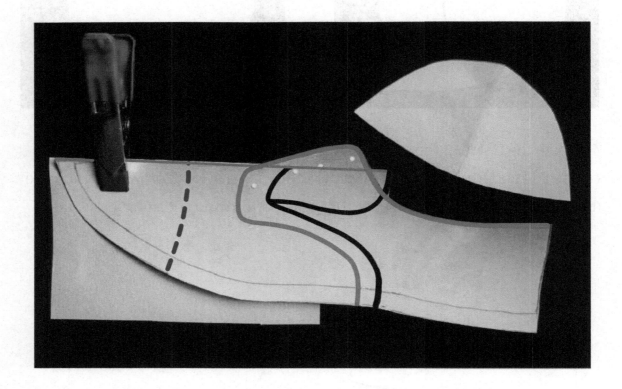

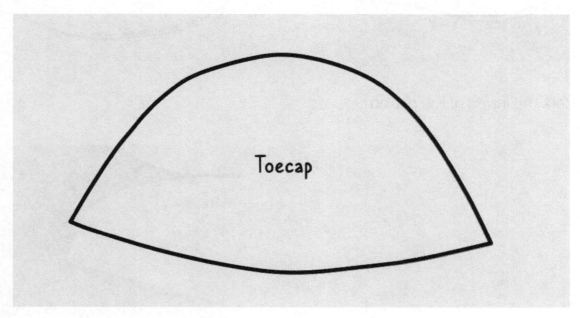

Toecap

Back strap

Cut out a piece of paper the same length as the back curve of the quarter. Fold the paper and draw the following measurements: 14 mm wide at the top, 8 mm wide at 1/3 distance down from the top, and 18 mm wide at the bottom.

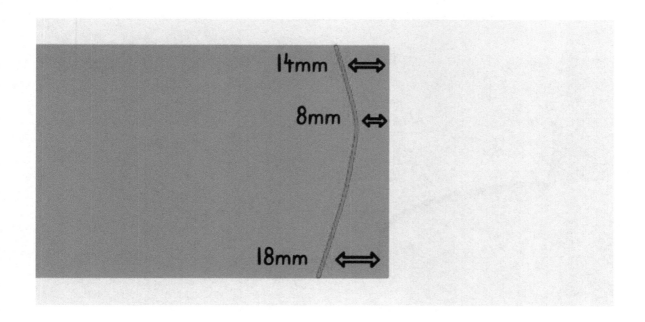

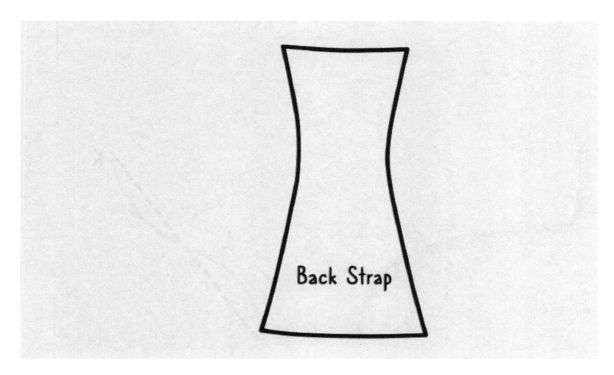

Outside Counter

An outside counter is an additional design element, it is not necessary but you might want to play with it one day. Of course, different designs are possible, this is just one version you could try out.

1. To create the outside counter mark the following reference points on the quarter: **K** is 12 mm from the upper corner of the quarter, **D** which is 1/4 of the SLL, and **L** which is halfway between **K** and **D**.

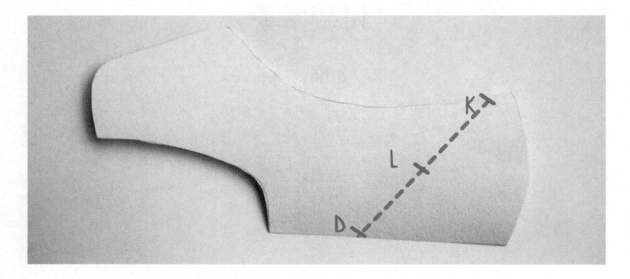

2. Draw in the counter line using the reference points as a guide.

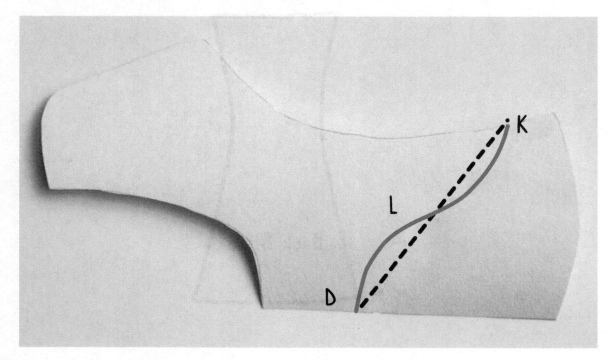

3. Place the counter on a folded piece of paper, back curve to the fold, meeting the fold about halfway up. Draw around the shape. Cut the counter out and label it.

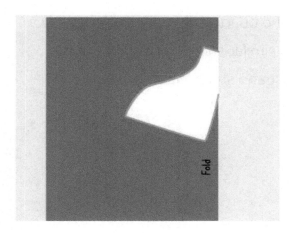
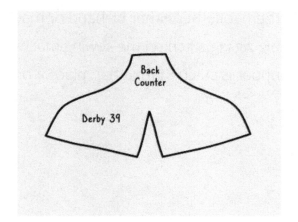

You now have all the pattern pieces you need to make the Derby shoe!

Step 3: Create the sole pattern

Create a sole pattern as described on page 69. Transfer all the pattern pieces onto thin cardboard, I often use cereal boxes, to make them sturdier.

Step 4: Create a mock-up

Cut your pattern pieces out of felt or other tightly woven fabric. The sole can also be cut from felt or use cardboard to get a stiffer sole. For the correct placement of the quarters check page 110. Secure the pieces with a few pins. Then sew them together either by hand or machine. The quarters join edge to edge, try a big zigzag stitch on the sewing machine or a similar stitch by hand. Once the upper is stitched together, place it on the last and stitch the sole.

Now hopefully, the mock-up fits the last perfectly. Take the shell off and try it on your foot. If everything is fine, you can start transferring your pattern pieces onto the leather, as described in the next step. Sometimes, if the foot is slimmer than the last, the gap between the facings has to be adjusted by trimming a few millimetres off the front edges of the facing.

If you find the shell sits a bit loose around your foot, it could be that the last is designed for an extra insole. In that case, once your shoes are completed, insert an insole. Cut it from 2 - 3 mm thick leather. If there are any other issues, you may have to go back through the previous steps again.

Step 5: Cut out leather pattern pieces

Transfer the vamp pattern pieces, the quarters and the back straps onto your upper leather. You can transfer your sole pattern onto the same leather or use other veg-tan leather for the top sole. Transfer the pattern of the sole onto thicker leather for the midsole. Cut out the leather pattern pieces according to the instructions on page 73.

Step 6: Make a toe puff and heel stiffener

Create a toe puff and heel stiffener as described on pages 80 - 83.

Step 7: Create stitching grooves

Create stitching grooves according to the instructions on page 94. Decide how you want to stitch on your quarters and drag the channels accordingly. A few options are shown on pages 110 - 111.

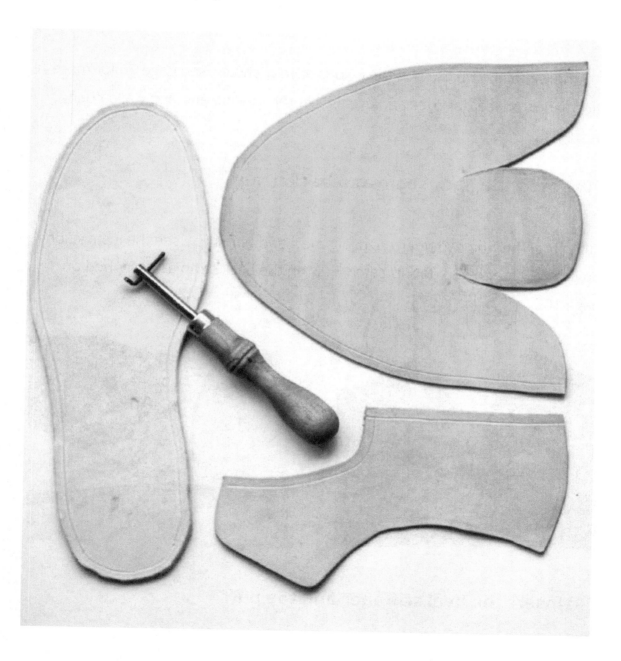

Step 8: Punch the stitching holes

Punch stitching holes see page 96 for how to do that. Punch the eyelet holes as well.

Step 9: Dye the leather pieces

Dye the vamp and quarters in the colour of your choice, see page 76 for more information on leather dyes and dyeing. Let the dye dry and apply a leather finish.

Step 10: Stitch the back seam and backstrap

Stitch together the two quarters using the x and bar stitch, see the instructions on page 98 for how to do this stitch. Sew on the back strap as described on page 106.

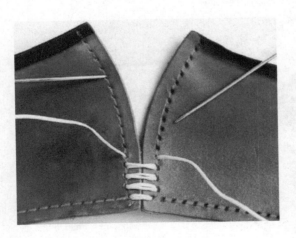 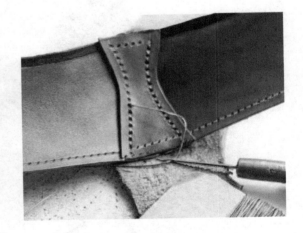

Step 11: Insert the heel stiffener and toe puff

With the water-based adhesive cement the heel stiffener to the quarters and the toe puff to the vamp (see pages 84 - 85).

Step 12: Line the upper

Cut out the lining according to the instructions on page 88 and cement it onto your upper pieces.

Step 13: Stitch the quarters to the vamp

Stitch the quarters to the vamp, see page 110 for more information.

Step 14: Last your shoes

Last your shoes as described in the chapter on lasting (pages 112 /13).

Step 15: Stitch the upper to the soles

Stitch the uppers to the soles (page120) using the lockstitch (page 100).

Step 16: Attach the outsoles

Attach the outsoles, see page 122 for instructions.

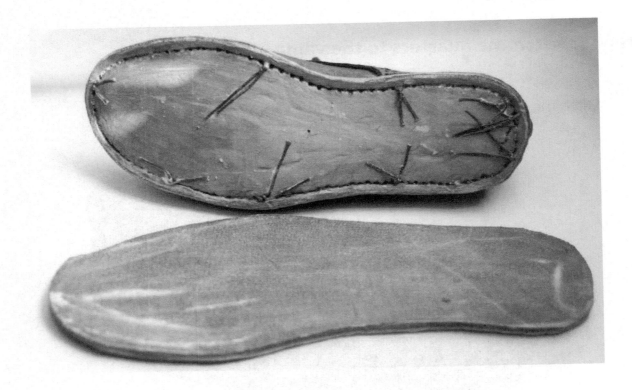

Step 17: Attach the heels

Attach the heels following the instructions on page 128.

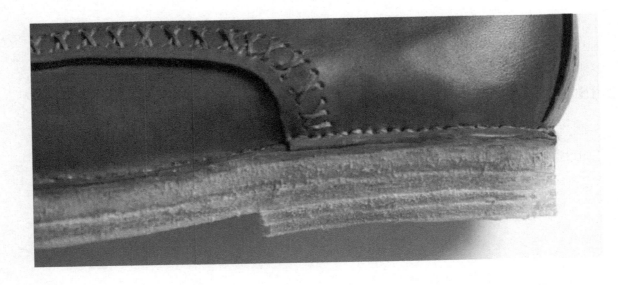

Step 18: Edge finish the soles

Edge finish the soles using the methods described on page 136.

Step 19: Crack the lasts

Crack the lasts as described on page 142.

Variation Of The Derby Shoe Pattern

This project is a variation of the above shoes to show how you can make a few changes to a pattern and produce a very different shoe.

I used calf hide leather (1.3 mm) and dyed it with Identity leather store water-based stain, brick red for the upper and chocolate brown for the edges. As an embellishment, I chose a pyramid and small dome-shaped studs (antique brass finish). I changed the quarter pattern to two pairs of eyelets and gave the French curve a twist. The vamp pattern is cut into 3 parts with a triangle shape added to it.

The construction method is the same as described for the shoes in the previous chapter. The only additional step is sewing on a toecap which consists of three parts in this case.

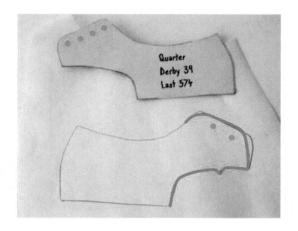 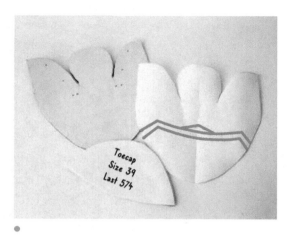

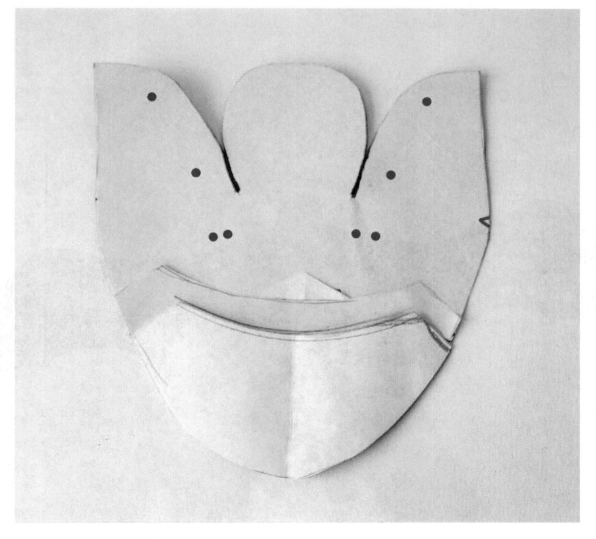

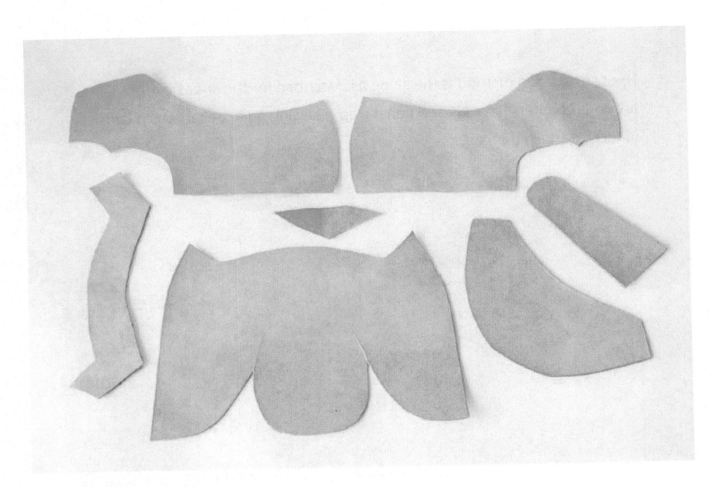

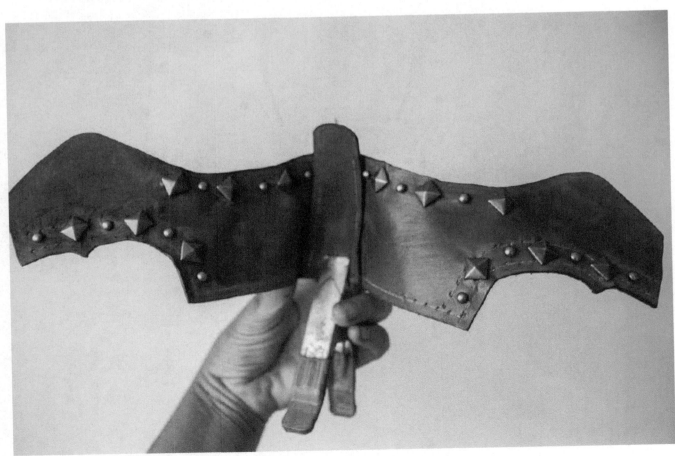

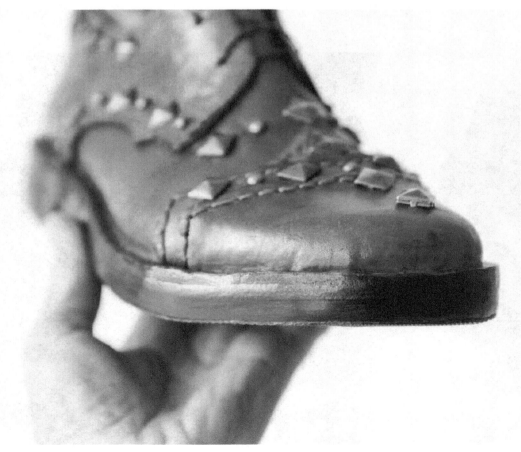

8-Eyelet Derby Boot

This is an ankle boot version of the Derby shoes. For elegant-looking boots, choose calfskin leather for sturdier work boots cowhide. The 8-eyelet boots have a height of about 14 cm, measured from the sole edge. You can make them shorter when designing the pattern. For longer boots, there is a better-suited pattern construction method which I describe in the chapter on making 14 eyelet boots.

I used cowhide (1 mm) to make these boots. I dyed it with Identity leather store water-based stain (chocolate brown). The painted boots are made the same way as the brown boots. I used the same cowhide but dyed the leather green and then painted the pattern pieces with acrylic leather paint. I made plateau boots here using a thick midsole (8 mm). The soles are still flexible, and the boots are comfortable to walk in. But of course, you don't have to use a thick midsole 3 - 5 mm is absolutely fine.

To create the boot pattern you will need the mean form of the lasts you are using. For how to make one see the instructions in the chapter on pattern making.

Step 1: Creating the design standard for a Derby boot

1. **Draw around the mean form** onto thick paper and transfer the points **S**, **CP**, **V** and **I**. **Mark point J,** which is the joint position, the widest part of the front part: Use the mean form from before and transfer the point where the inside and outside lines cross point **J**.

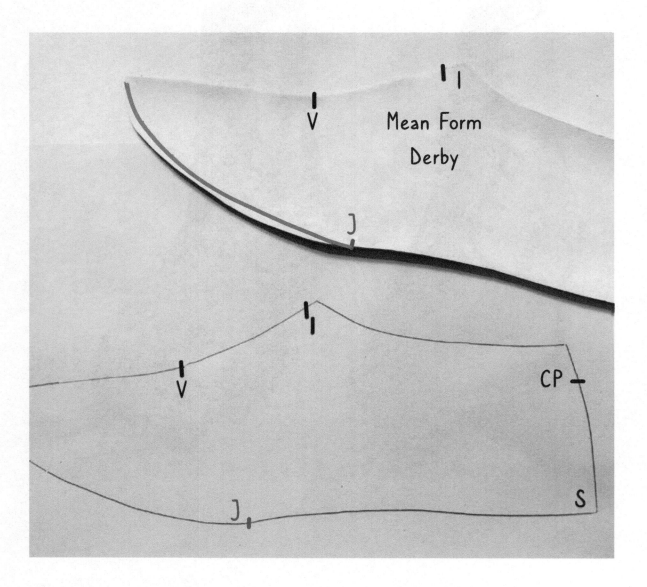

2. On a large sheet of paper (40 x 30 cm), draw a horizontal line **AB** and a vertical line at the right end about 15 cm high. Position your mean form inside these lines placing point **J** on the horizontal line and point **CP** on the vertical line to mark point **D** on the vertical line.

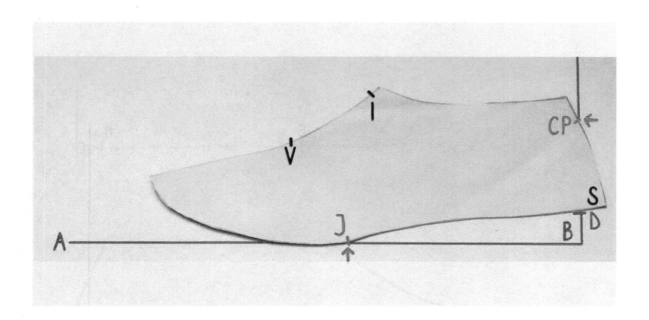

3. **Draw around the mean form** in the same position as the last step and mark point **C**, which is 13.6 cm from **D** on the vertical line.

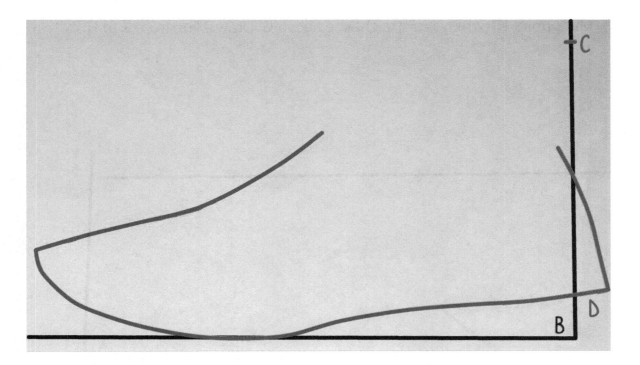

4. **Design the ankle girth:** Draw a parallel line to AB from point **C**. On this line, mark point H 6mm from **C** and then **G** 11 cm from **H**. Of course, you can take measurements if you have a wider-than-average ankle girth. Lay a tape measure around your ankle at the height of your boots and divide that number by 2. Adjust the distance between **H** and **G** accordingly.

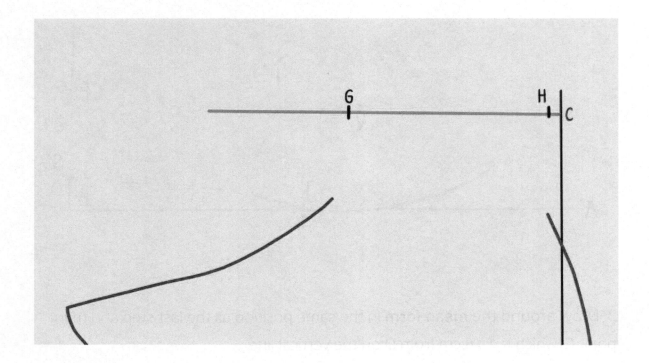

5. **Mark point K** 12 mm in a straight line above **G**. Draw a line from **K** to **H**.

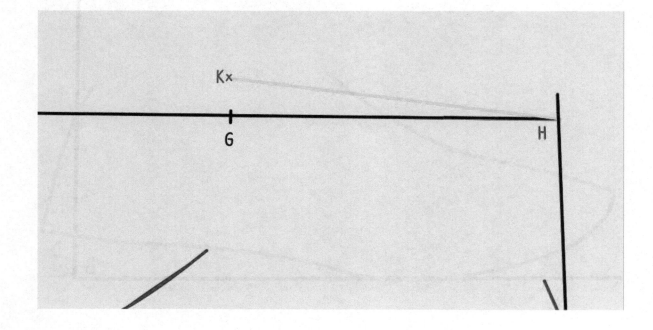

6. **Draw a fold line** from **V** to the top of the toe. Later we will fold the pattern along this centre line to create the full vamp.

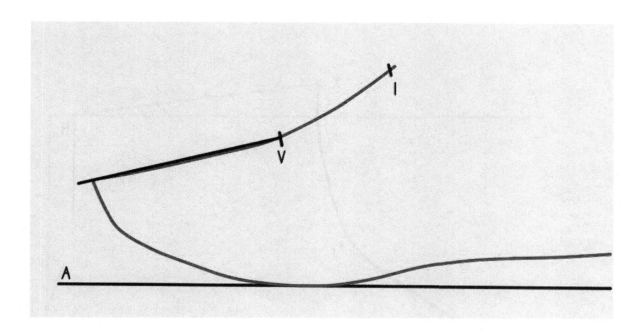

7. Draw a straight line from point **V** to point **I**.

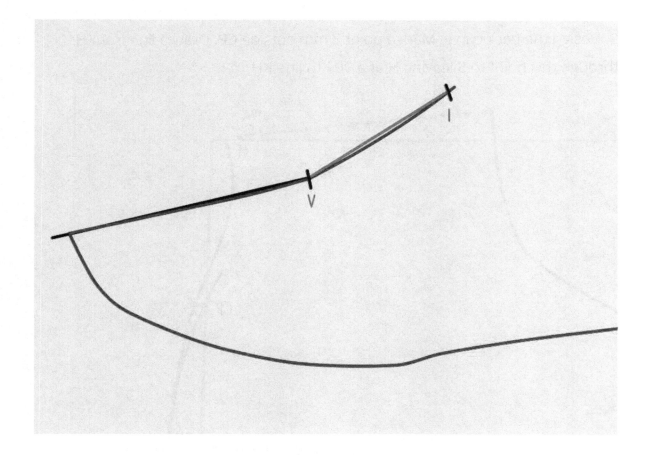

8. Design the front line of the standard: Mark a point 3 mm to the outside from point I. Draw a line passing through this point from V to K. The line between V and I has a very slight curve above the straight line.

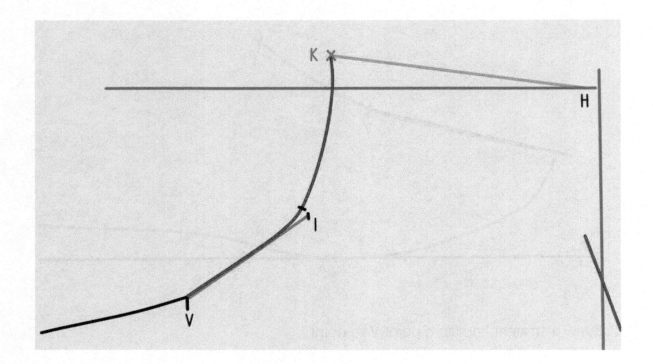

9. Design the back curve: Mark a point 3 mm outside CP. Draw a line from H through this point to S leaving H at a 90° to line KH.

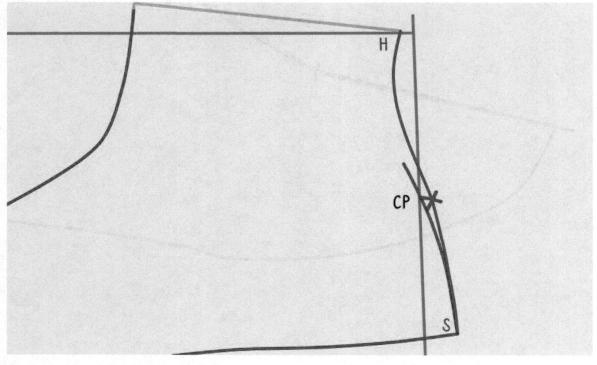

10. **Add the seam allowance** of 7 mm using a compass.

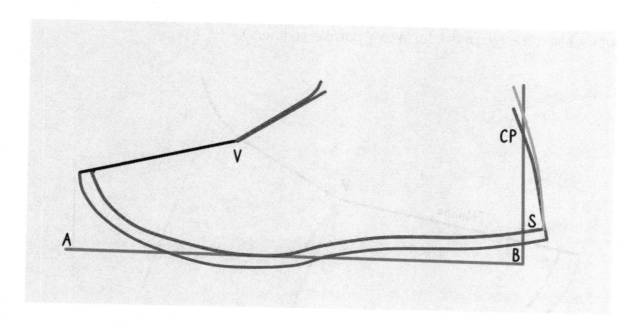

11. The outline of the ankle boot standard is now finished. The next step will be to **add the design lines**. Draw a line halfway down the form from **V**, at 90° to the fold line. Draw another line from **V** at 90° to line VI.

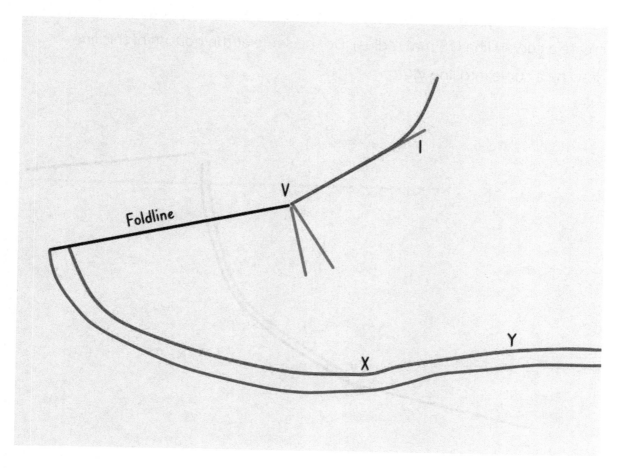

12. Now **draw a line through the middle of these two lines**, from **V** to the edge of the form to point **X**. This will be the front of the facing. Draw another line from point **I** to the edge of the form to **Y** parallel to line **VX**.

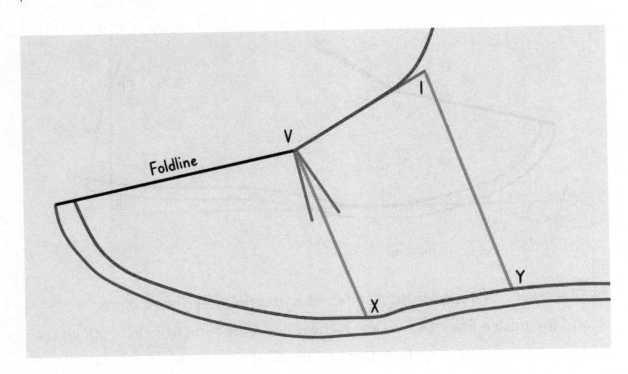

13. **Draw a line parallel to the front line V to K** 3 mm away. At the top of this line create a curved line (15 mm radius). Do the same at the bottom of this line drawing a curve into line **VX**.

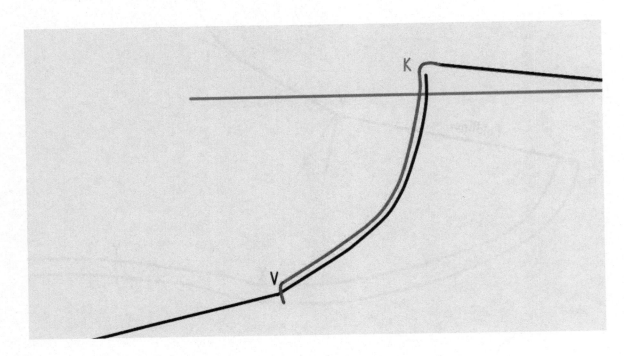

14. **Mark point V2** which is in the middle of line VX. Create the side-curve of the quarter starting at point **V2** passing through a point on the feather line about 10 mm behind point **Y**.

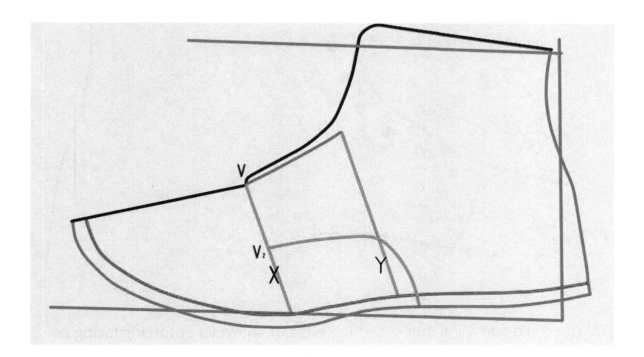

15. **Draw a line for the eyelets**. The line should be 11 mm from the edge of the quarter. Mark the beginning and end of the eyelet positions: at the bottom 8 mm from the front of the facing and at the top 8 mm from the line **KH**.

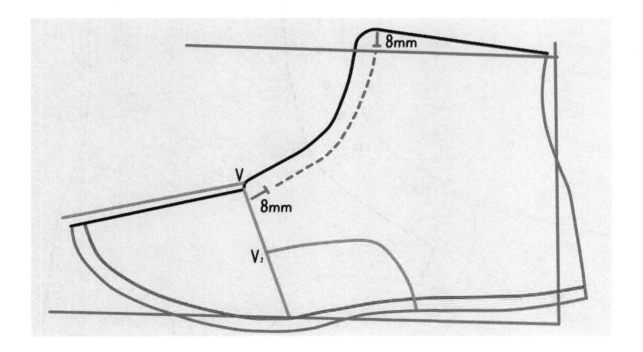

16. **Draw in the eyelet position**, about 15 mm apart, using a divider or compass for even spacing.

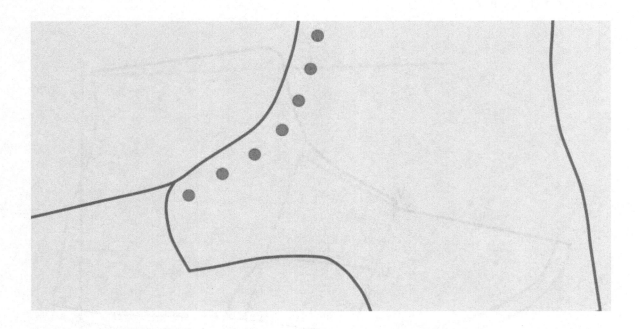

17. You could add a line that shows the **edge of an eyelet enforcing facing** or marks the stitching line that secures a facing. Draw this line 23 mm in from the edge of the quarter.

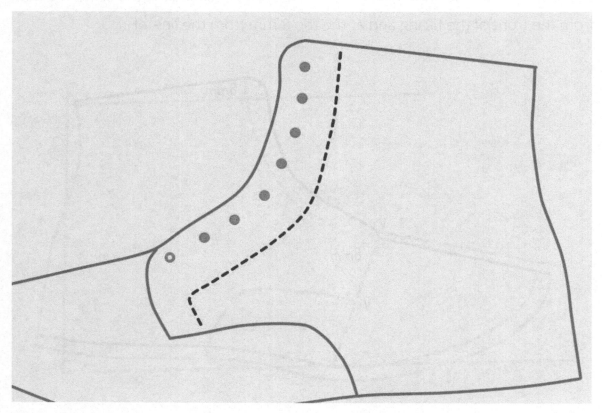

18. You could also add the line for a **toecap** see page 166, and a line for an **outside counter** (page 168).

19. **Cut the standard out** and write down all the important information.

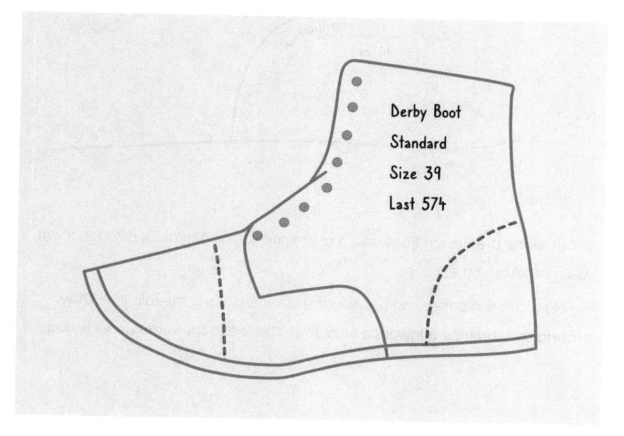

Derby Boot

Standard

Size 39

Last 574

Step 2: Cutting sectional patterns

Vamp And Quarter

1. Follow the steps 14 and 15 on pages 156/57 to add the **vamp underlay**.

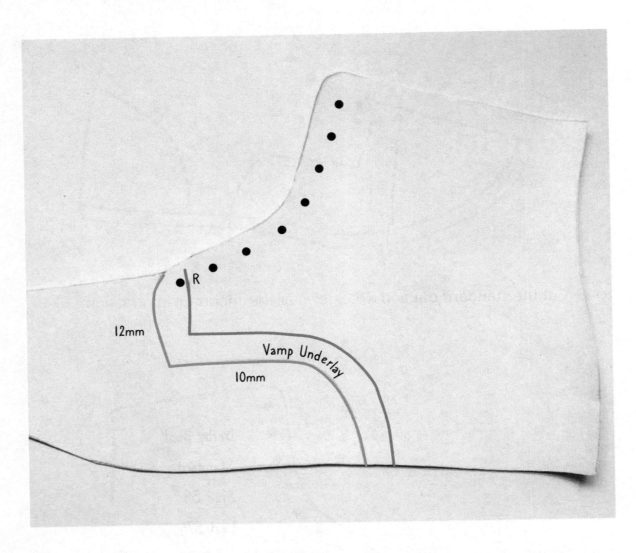

2. **Cut along the design lines** with a craft knife so you can mark through them when producing the vamp.

3. Fold a piece of paper and position the standard along the fold line. **Draw around the stitching allowance** edge from the toe to the vamp underlay line.

4. Mark through the vamp underlay line from **R** to the edge of the stitching allowance.

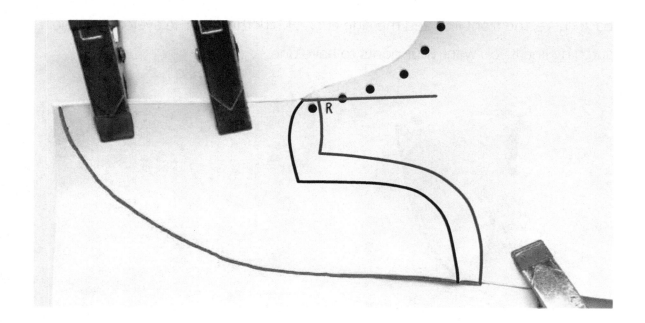

5. Pierce through the quarter shape at each point shown with a cross using a nail or other sharp tool.

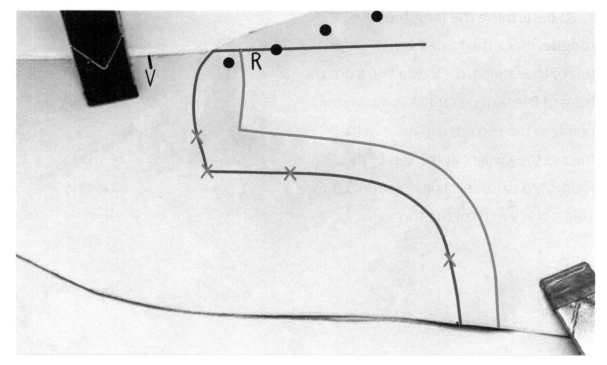

6. **Create the inside of the vamp pattern**, as described in step 4 on page 165. Mark the piercings and cut out the pattern.

7. **Cut out the quarter** from the standard and place it on paper. Draw along the back curve, the front line and the side curve. Mark through the eyelets and the stitching line if you want your boots to have one.

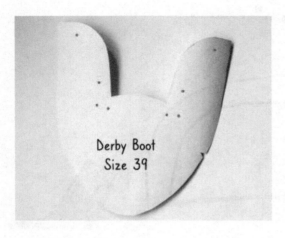
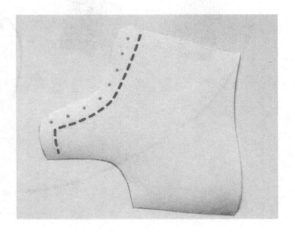

The Tongue

1. To **determine the length of the tongue,** place the folded vamp pattern on top of the standard. Draw a line from the base of the tongue (at the vamp throat point) to the top edge in a curve that follows the eyelets at the top of the facing. Measure this line and add 5 mm. This is the length of the tongue.

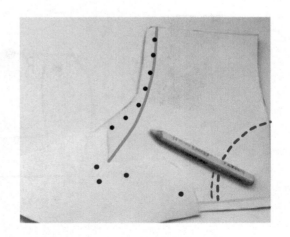

2. Fold a piece of paper and place the vamp onto this paper, fold on fold. Draw the base of the tongue. **Measure and mark the tongue** length and the width as shown in the photo, 32 mm at its widest part and 25 mm towards the top. Design your tongue according to these measurements. Cut the shape out.

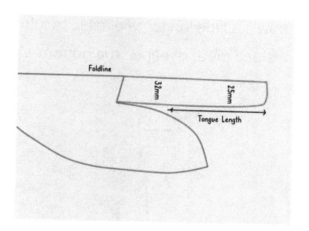

3. Tape the tongue to the vamp and **glue the pattern onto thin cardboard** to make a sturdier pattern.

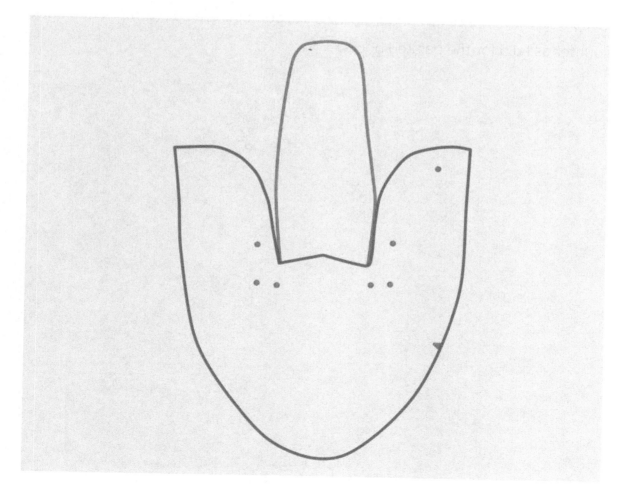

Back Strap

The height of the back strap is the same length as the back-curve line. You could draw it a little longer to be able to fold it in for a pull tab. Design the back strap on a folded piece of paper, the bottom width is 22 mm the top 8 mm.

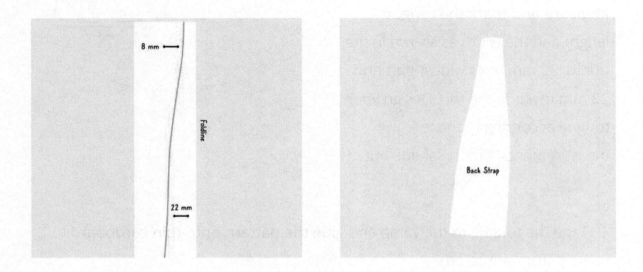

Of course, there are different possibilities like combining a back strap with a back counter as I did for the painted boots.

Step 3: Create the sole pattern

Create a sole pattern as described on page 69. Transfer all the pattern pieces onto thin cardboard,

Step 4: Create a mock up

If you don't have a boot last, adjust your last to resemble a boot form see page 35 for how to do that.

Create a mock-up. Place the vamp, quarter and sole onto felt fabric. Cut the pieces out and secure them with a few pins. Then stitch them together either by hand or machine. The quarters join edge to edge, try a big zigzag stitch on the sewing machine or a similar stitch by hand. Once you have the upper stitched together, place it on the last and stitch the sole on.

Step 5: Cut out the leather pieces

Decide if you want a toecap before cutting out the pattern pieces. If so, adjust the vamp pattern as described on page 109. Cut the pattern pieces out of your leather as described on page 73.

Step 6: Make a toe puff and heel stiffener

Make a toe puff according to the instructions on page 80. Decide if you want to enforce the heel section with an appliqué heel counter which does not need a heel stiffener or if you want to sew on a back strap which would need a heel stiffener.

Step 7: Create stitching grooves

Create stitching grooves on the pattern pieces and top sole, see page 94 for more details.

Step 8: Punch stitching holes

Punch the stitching holes according to the instructions on page 96.

Step 9: Dye the leather

Dye the leather. Check page 76 for more information on dyeing.

Step 10: Stitch back seam and back strap

Stitch the quarters together using the x and bar stitch page 98. Stitch the backstrap on following instructions on page 104.

Step 11: Stitch the toecap on

Skive the vamp front edge and stitch the toecap onto the vamp.

Step 12: Add a toe puff and heel stiffener

Cement the toe puff onto the vamp and the heel stiffener, if using, onto the stitched together quarters following instructions on pages 80 - 85.

Step 13: Line the upper

Cut out the lining from your chosen material and cement the lining onto vamp and quarters following instructions on pages 86 - 89.

Step 14: Set the eyelets

Set the eyelets if using, see page 90 for more details.

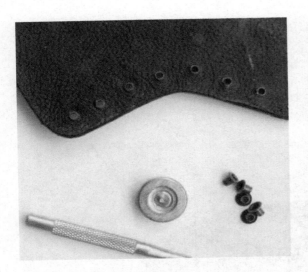 

Step 15: Stitch the quarters onto the vamp

Stitch the quarters onto the vamp according to instructions on page 110.

Step 16: Last the boots

Last the boots following instructions on page 112.

Step 17: Stitch the Uppers to the Soles

Stitch the uppers to the soles following the instructions on page 120 using the lockstitch (page100).

Step 18: Attach the outsoles

Follow the instructions on page 122 for how to attach the outsoles.

Step 19: Attach the heels

Attach the heels as described on page 128.

Step 20: Edge finish the soles

Edge finish the soles as described on page 136.

Step 21: Crack the lasts

Crack the lasts as described on page 142.

14-Eyelet Derby Boots

These boots feature a slim high-rise style and are great for wearing with skirts. I embellished them with studs and dyed the leather with a black water-based stain.

The construction of the boots is very similar to the 8-eyelets boots. Although I am using a different method for making the pattern, which is more suitable for high-rise boots.

You can use this pattern-making method for all boots with more than 8 pairs of eyelets. The 14-eyelet boots are 20 cm high. I recommend using boot hooks for the upper 4 pairs of eyelets. They will make getting in and out of the shoes easier.

I tried to find some with an antique silver finish, as all the other metal studs I used on these boots have this finish, but I wasn't successful in my search, so I went with the eyelets all the way up. Learn from my mistake and gather all your metal finishes before starting a project to be sure everything you want for your boots is available.

For these boots, I used an oiled calf hide leather (1.3 mm) and dyed it with a black water-based stain.

You will need the mean form constructed in the chapter on pattern making and a 180° protractor to create this boot pattern.

Step 1: Creating the 14 eyelet boot pattern

1. **Draw around the mean form** on a piece of paper. Transfer the reference points **CP**, **S**, **V** and **I**. Draw a line from **CP** to **V**.

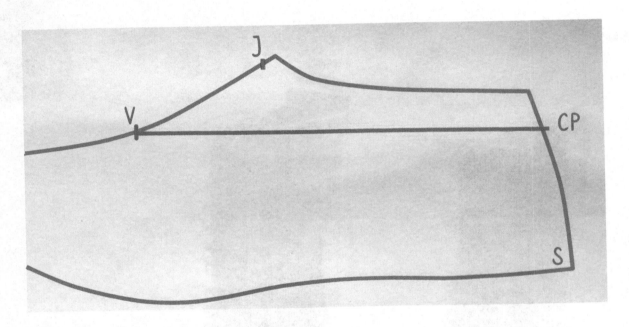

2. Draw a line at 76° to the line **CP** - **V**, from **V** to meet point **E** at the feather line.

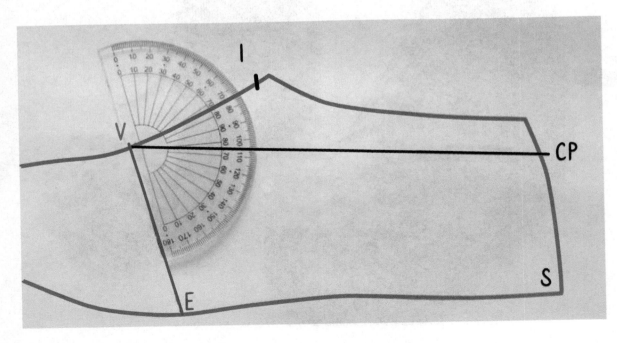

3. Draw a line from point **E** to point **S**.

Draw a line from point **E** to point **F**, 20mm down from point **S**.

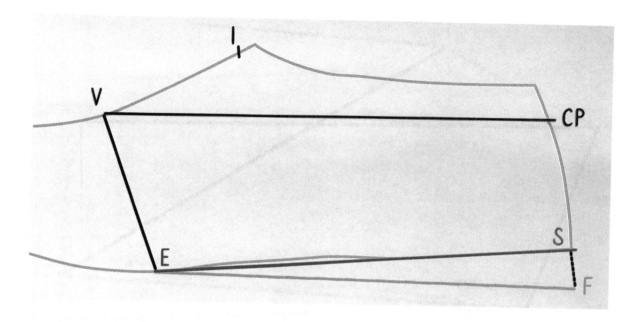

4. **Construct the leg height:** Draw a line from **S** to **I** and measure it.

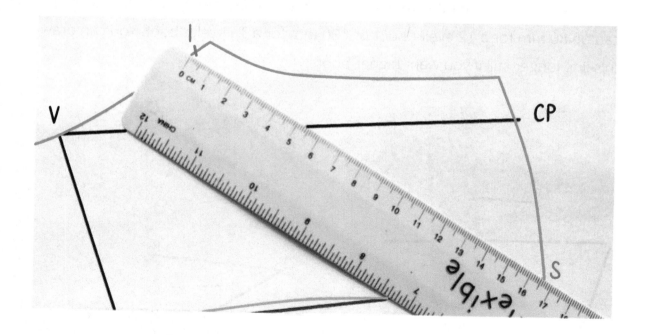

5. Draw a line from point I which is parallel to the line ES towards the back. Mark point **H** which is at half the length of line **I** - **S**.

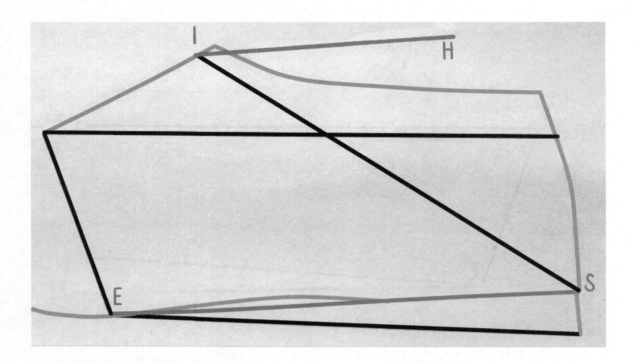

6. Draw a line from point H that is 90° to line EF. Mark point **K** on this line. This can be 80 mm for a 12 eyelet boot or 100 mm for a 14 eyelet boot. You can draw this line longer still if you want higher boots.

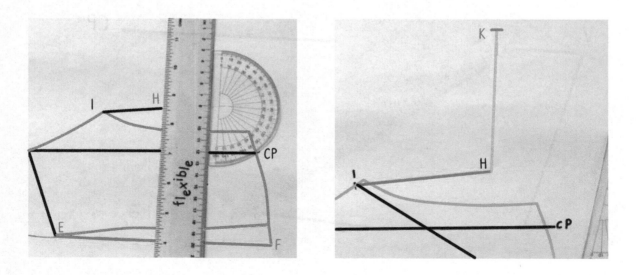

7. Draw a line which will be the top of the boot at 84° to line **HK**.

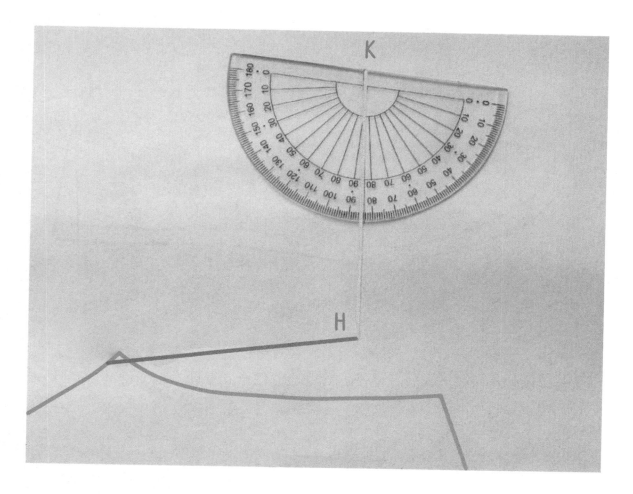

8. **Mark point L at the front and M at the back.** These are 61 mm for a 14-eyelet boot (59 mm for a 12-eyelet boot) from point **K**. If you don't have a standard leg width, take your own measurement. The 14-eyelet boot is 20 cm high. This is the height at which you have to measure the girth of your leg. Add 15 mm for the opening.

The lines **LK** and **KM** should always be the same length.

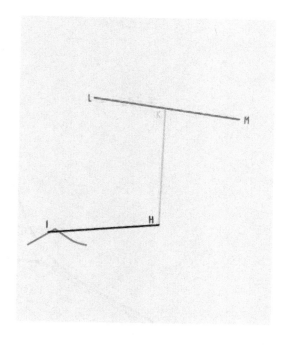

9. Add a seam allowance of 7mm using a compass.

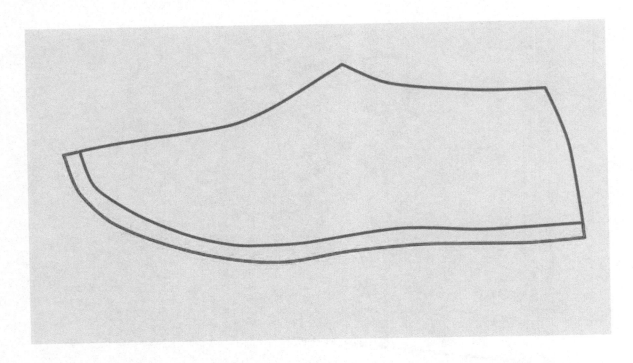

10. Draw the front curve from **V** passing point **I** 3 mm away, ending at point **L** at 90° to the line **LK**.

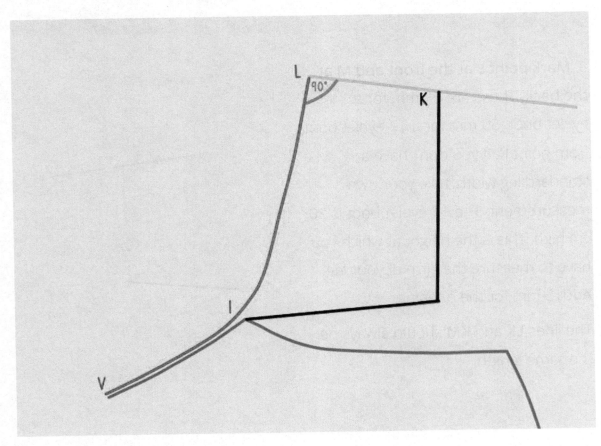

11. **Draw the back line** starting from M passing CP 3mm away. See the photo for the shape of the curve. Pass through S. Keep the shape of the curve until you meet the edge of the seam allowance.

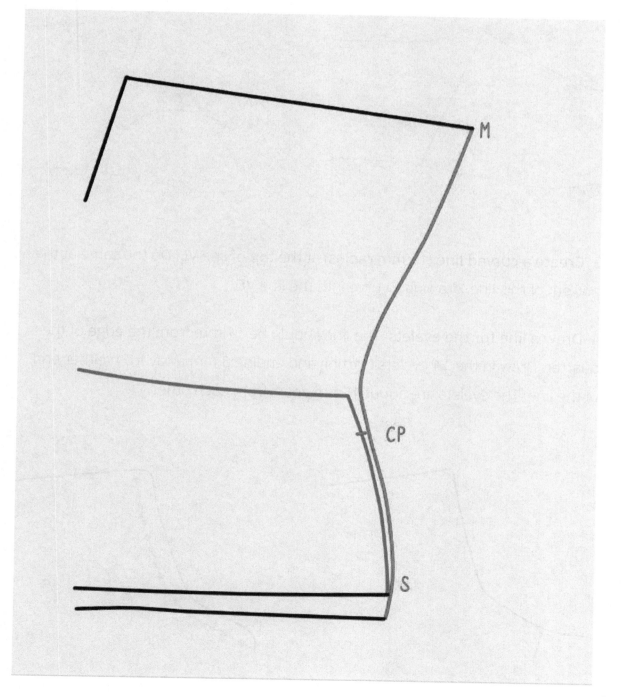

Adding the design lines

1. **Draw a line from point I to the edge of the form to Y** parallel to the line **VE**.

2. **Create the side-curve of the quarter:** Start in the middle of line **VE** passing through a point on the feather line about 1 cm before point **Y**. I am making a shorter side curve here than in the previous patterns if you would prefer a longer one, end the line 10mm behind point **Y**.

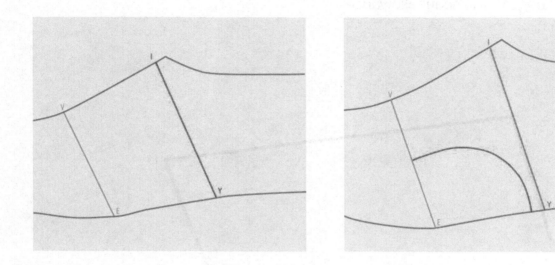

3. **Create a curved line** (15 mm radius) at the top of line **VL**. Do the same at the bottom of this line, drawing a curve into the line **VE**.

4. **Draw a line for the eyelets**. The line should be 11 mm from the edge of the quarter. Draw in the 14 eyelets starting and ending 8 mm away from either end of the line. The eyelets are about 15mm apart from each other.

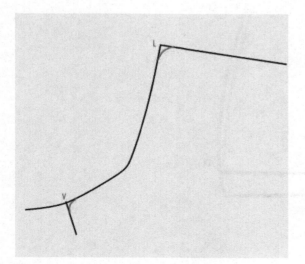

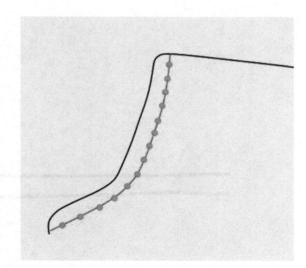

5. Cut out the standard and write down last, size and design.

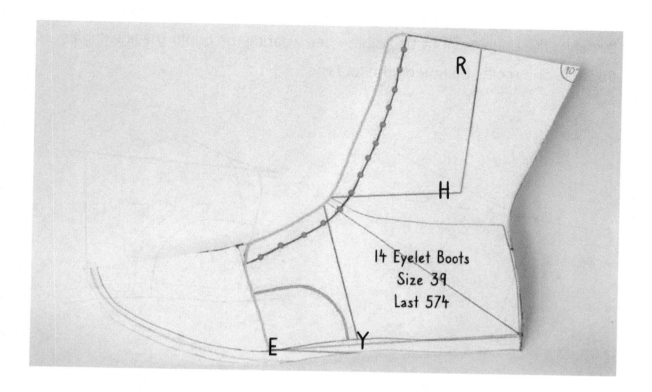

Step 2: Cutting sectional patterns

Vamp

1. **Extend the crease line** to beyond the quarter line.

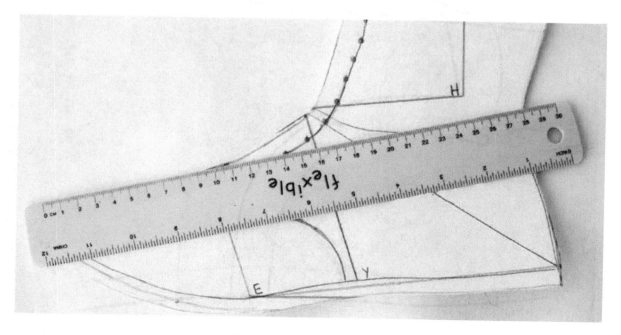

2. **Mark point R which** is 25 mm along this line from **V**.

3. **Draw a 10 mm underlay line.** The underlay is increased to 12 mm in the throat so the opening won't be visible when wearing the boots. The line curves upwards and meets point **R** on the fold line.

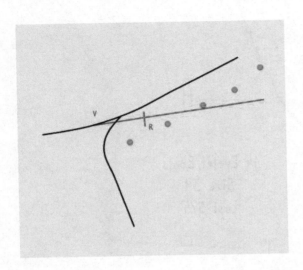 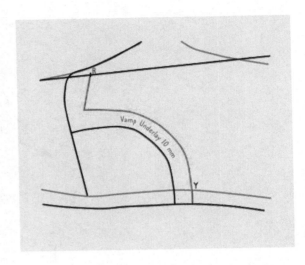

4. **Cut along the design lines** so you can mark through them when producing the vamp.

5. **Pierce through the quarter shape** at each x-point, using an awl or other sharp tool.

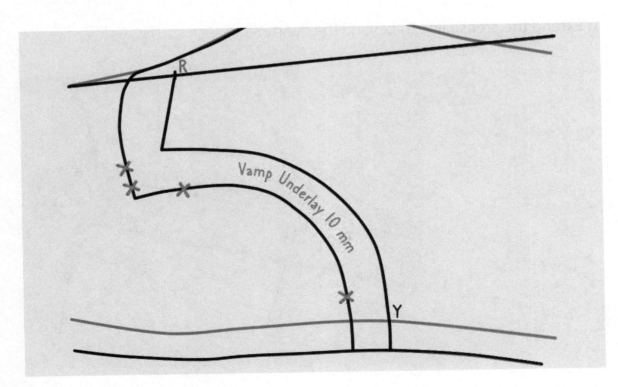

6. Fold a piece of paper and position the standard along the fold line. Draw around the stitching allowance edge from the toe to the vamp underlay line. Mark through the vamp underlay line from **R** to the edge of the stitching allowance. Mark through the piercings.

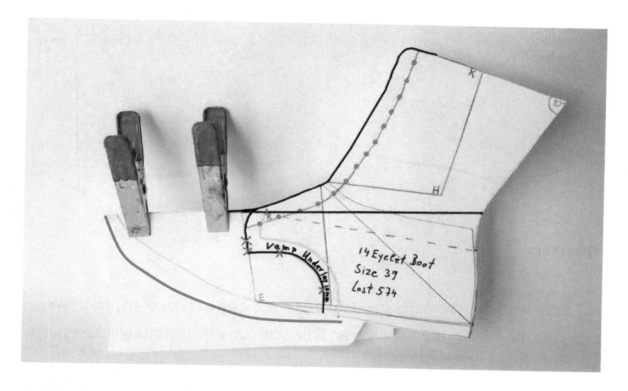

7. Cut out the vamp.

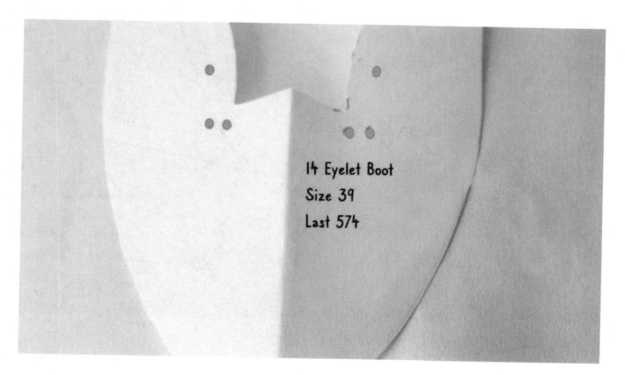

8. Create the inside of the vamp pattern: Position your Mean Form along the crease line and transfer point J onto the vamp pattern. Next, draw the inside line (red line on the Mean Form) onto the vamp pattern and cut along it. Mark the inside with a v at the edge.

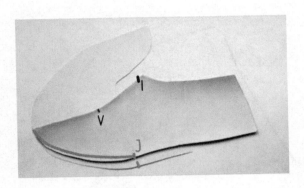 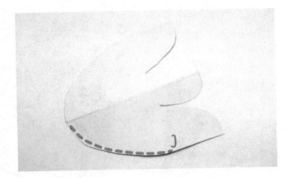

Quarters

Cut out the quarter from the standard and place it on a sheet of paper. Draw along the back curve, the front line and the side curve. Mark through the eyelets.

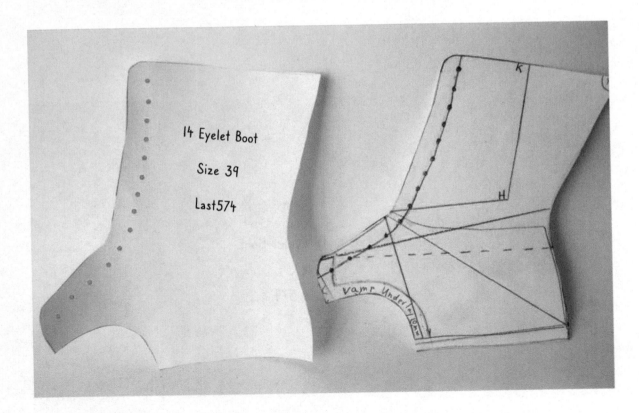

The Tongue

1. To determine the length of the tongue places the folded vamp pattern on top of the standard. Draw a line from the base (at the vamp throat point) to the top edge in a curve that follows the eyelets at the upper part of the facing. Measure this line and add 5 mm.

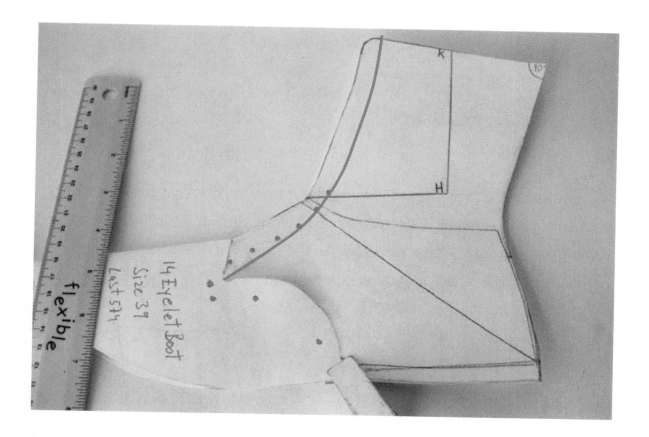

2. Fold a piece of paper and place the folded vamp onto this paper, fold on fold. Draw the base of the tongue. Measure and mark the tongue length and the width as shown in the photo, 32 mm at its widest part and 25 mm towards the top, and design your tongue according to these measurements. Cut out the tongue. Attach the vamp to the tongue

The Back Strap

Draw the pattern for the back strap on a folded piece of paper. The height of the back strap has the same length as the back-curve line. Mine is 22mm wide at the bottom and 8 mm at the top.

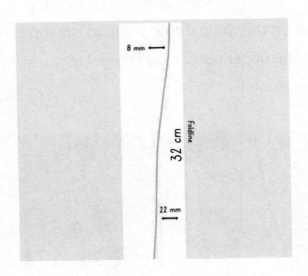 

If you would like a toecap, check page 158 for how to construct one. For a heel counter, check page 168. Once you have a toecap, draw the top line onto the vamp pattern adding 10mm underlay. Do the same with the back counter pattern. Cut out the new vamp and quarter patterns.

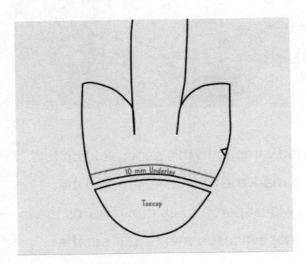 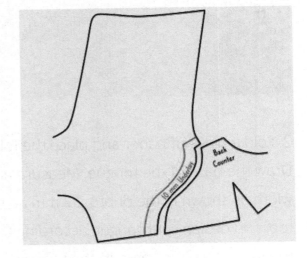

Once you have all the pattern pieces glue them onto thin cardboard and cut them out.

Step 3: Create the sole pattern

Create a sole pattern as described on page 69. Transfer all the pattern pieces onto thin cardboard.

Step 4: Adjust your last and create a mock up

If you don't have a boot last, adjust your last to resemble a boot form. See page 35 for how to do that. Create a mock-up as described on page 170.

Step 5: Cut out the leather pieces

Cut the pattern pieces out of your leather as described on page 73.

Step 6: Make a toe puff and heel stiffener

Make a toe puff according to the instructions on pages 80 - 86. Decide if you want to enforce the heel section with an appliqué heel counter which does not need a heel stiffener, or prefer to sew on a back strap which would require a heel stiffener.

Step 7: Create stitching grooves

Create stitching grooves on the pattern pieces and top sole, see page 94 for more details.

Step 8: Decorate the toecaps

If you want to decorate your toecap with metal studs make a pattern for the placement of the studs. Dye the toecaps and add the studs. It is best to buy the studs in a kit to make sure you have the right setting tools for them. I am using dome-shaped rivets and spike studs.

Step 9: Punch stitching holes

Punch the stitching holes according to the instructions on page 96.

Step 10: Dye the leather

Dye the remaining leather pieces. Check page 76 for more information on dyeing leather.

Step 11: Stitch the toecap on

Skive the front vamp edge and sew the toecap to the vamp.

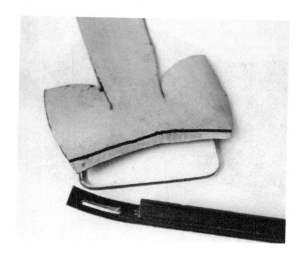 

Prepare the quarters: Skive the edges as marked on the picture below, dye all the pieces and punch the stitching holes.

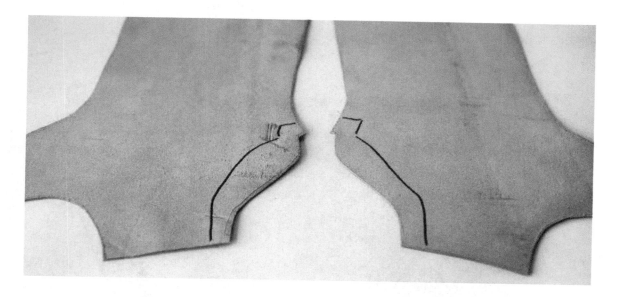

Step 12: Stitch the back seam and back strap

If you like, add some dome shaped studs to the back counter. Stitch the back quarters together with the x and bar stitch (page 104). Stitch the back counter on.

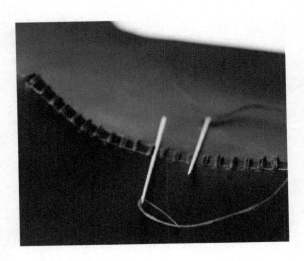 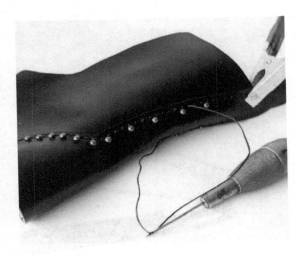

Step 13: Add a toe puff and heel stiffener

Cement the toe puff onto the vamp and the heel stiffener onto stitched together quarters following instructions on pages 84/5.

Step 14: Line the upper

Line the quarters and vamp (pages 86 - 89).

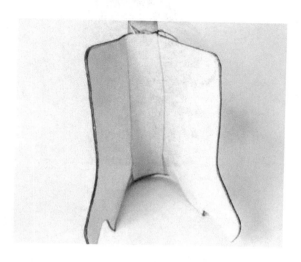 

Dye the lining or leave as is. Burnish all edges except the bottom edges which will be burnished at a later stage.

Stitch down the pull tab or use a rivet like I did here.

Step 15: Set the eyelets

Punch the holes for the eyelets and set them with metal eyelets (page 90).

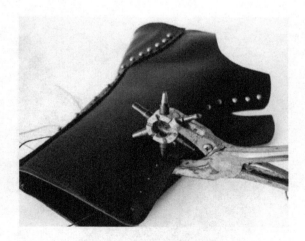 

Step 16: Stitch the quarters onto the vamp

Prepare this step by transferring the markings of the vamp placement you made earlier onto the leather. Hold the quarter in place with a clasp or double sided tape and stitch it onto the vamp.

 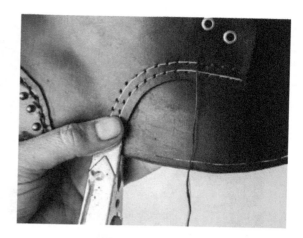

Step 17: Last the boots

Last the boots following instructions on page 112.

Step 18: Stitch the uppers to the soles

Stitch the uppers to the soles following the instructions on page 126.

Step 19: Attach the outsoles

Follow instructions on page 122 for how to attach the outsoles.

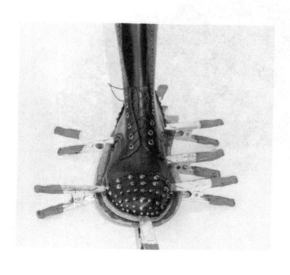 

Step 20: Attach the heels

Attach the heels, see page 128 for more details.

Step 21: Edge finish the soles

Finish the sole edges as described on page 136.

Step 22: Crack the lasts

Crack the lasts as described on page 142.

Here is a variation of the 14-eyelet boot pattern. I used 2 kinds of boot lace hooks and lined the boots with rabbit skin. These are very cosy winter boots.

Half-Bellows Tongue

A bellows tongue is a tongue/facing-lining unit stitched to the side of the boot. It allows the shoe to expand or contract like the bellows used to increase the flame in a blacksmith's forge as the laces are loosened and tightened. A bellows tongue boot has several unique qualities: It accommodates a variety of widths of feet and legs and prevents water from getting into a lace-up boot.

The following steps describe how to make the pattern for a half-bellow tongue which is joined to the facing lining for half the length of the tongue at each side (in contrast to a full-bellows tongue which is attached to the facing lining for all its length). Depending on the height of the boots you want to make, choose either the 8-eyelet or the 14-eyelet boot pattern as the base pattern for the bellows tongue.

Apart from the bellows tongue, I added a strap closure to the boots shown here, and I will describe briefly how I went about it. The construction method is the same as described in the boot-making chapters. I used cowhide leather (1mm) and dyed it with Giardini water-based dye (dark red), and finished it with a gloss finish.

Designing the half bellow tongue pattern

The starting point for making the half-bellow tongue pattern is the boot standard created for either the 8-eyelet or the 14-eyelet boots. I am using the 8-eyelet boot standard in this example. The shaded area and the tongue are joined together to design the pattern.

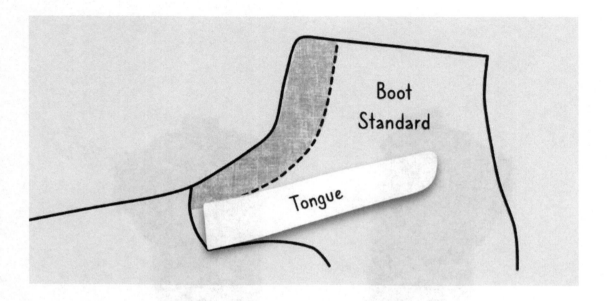

1. **Make a copy of the standard** and draw in the stitching line of the facing, the quarter lines and the fold line.

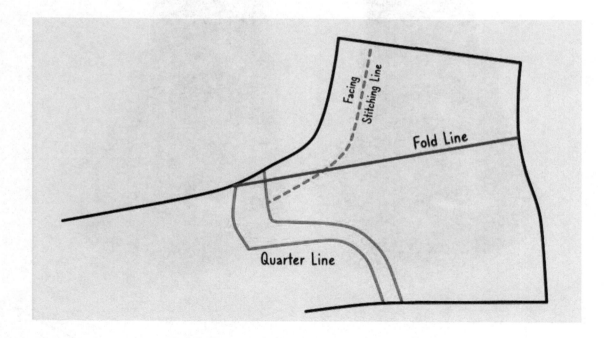

2. **Draw in the tongue** and find point **X** which is at the outer corner of the tongue as shown below (second picture).

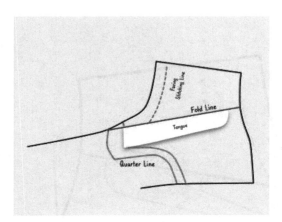 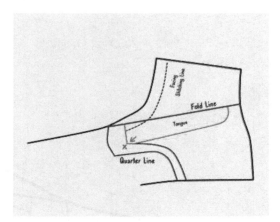

3. **Create the lines X to Y and X to Z:** They are about half the length of the tongue. These two lines have to be the same length and meet at point **X**. Between point **Y** and the facing, as well as between **Z** and the side of the tongue has to be a gap of about 10 - 15 mm, as indicated by the arrows below.

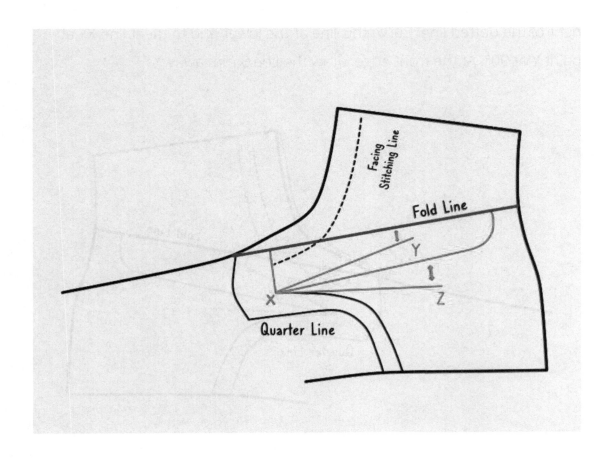

4. **Draw the line for the slit** of the facing from point **X** to a point just above the corner of the side curve line (pink).

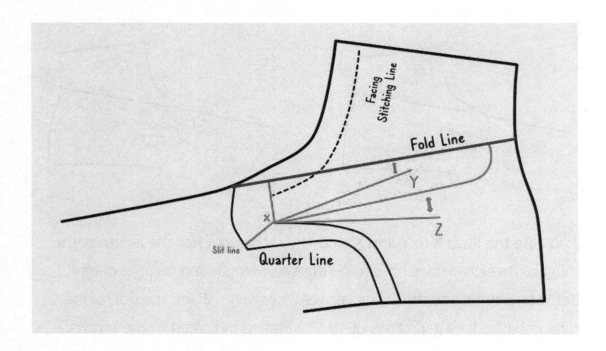

5. For the **facing**, draw a line at the top half of the facing about 6 mm to the right of the dotted line. Curve this line at the lower end to meet line **XY** at point **Y** at 90°. At the front edge, draw the line 3 mm away.

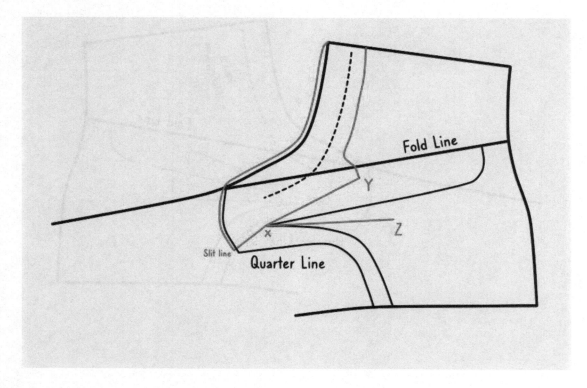

6. **For the tongue area**: Close the shape at point **Z** at 90°. Now copy the facing and tongue area onto tracing paper. Cut both shapes out.

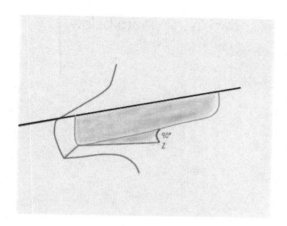
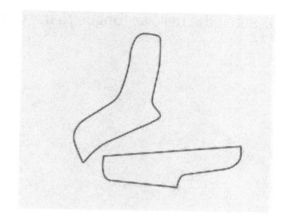

7. Lay the tongue and facing patterns on a folded piece of paper and draw around them. Cut the pattern out.

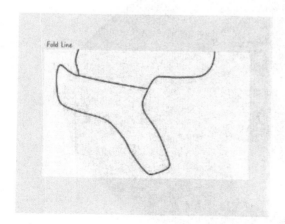
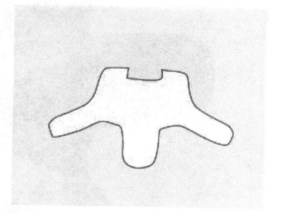

Attaching the half bellow tongue

The bellows tongue has to be made from soft and flexible leather. I used two layers of lining leather.

1. Stitch the bellows tongue to the vamp as shown in the photo below.

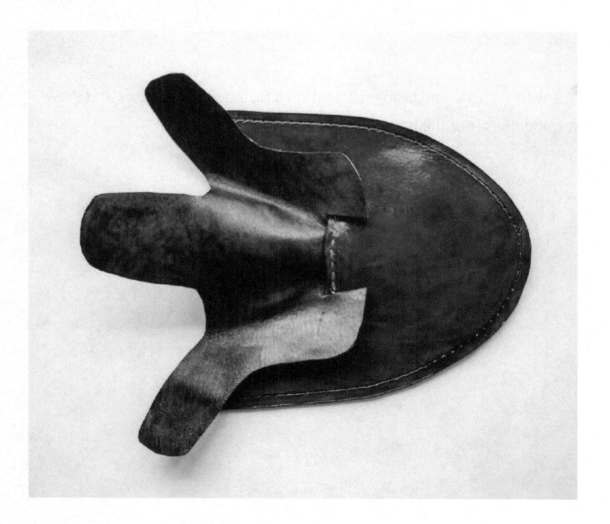

2. With a wing divider and the grooving tool add a groove to the facing stitching line. Punch holes along these grooves with the chisels.

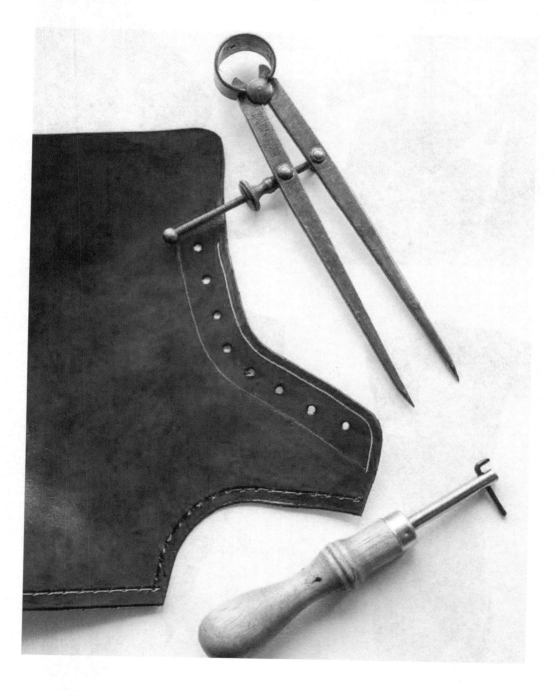

3. Stitch the tongue onto the quarters using double-sided tape or clamps to hold the tongue between the quarters while stitching.

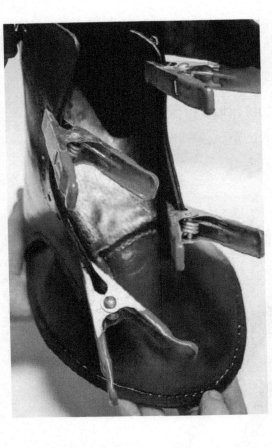

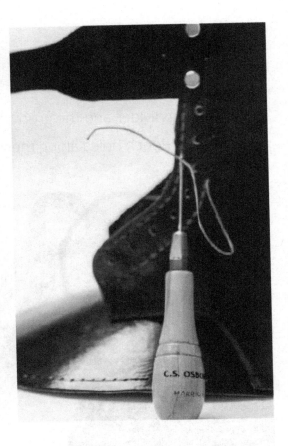

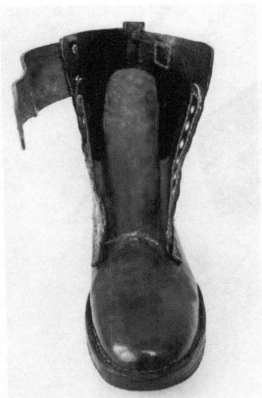

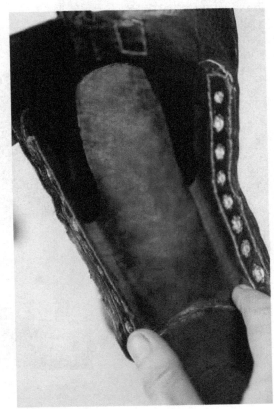

The Strap Closure

As a design variation, I added a strap closure to the 14-eyelet boot pattern. In case you would like to do something similar, here are a few photos showing how I added the straps. First, I punched a slit in the right quarter with a slot punch, dyed the edges of the slit and threaded the wider strap in.

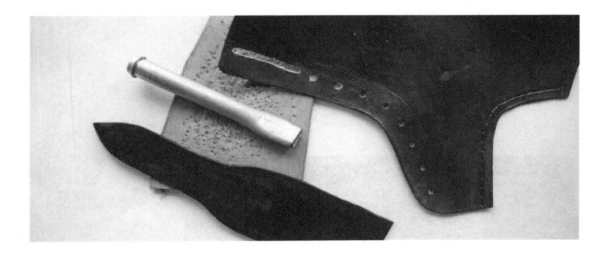

I then glued the lining in place and secured the sandwiched strap with two screw rivets.

For the other quarter, I prepared the strap that holds the buckle by punching a slit into it with a slot punch. If you don't have one, you could punch a hole at either end and make two cuts connecting the dots.

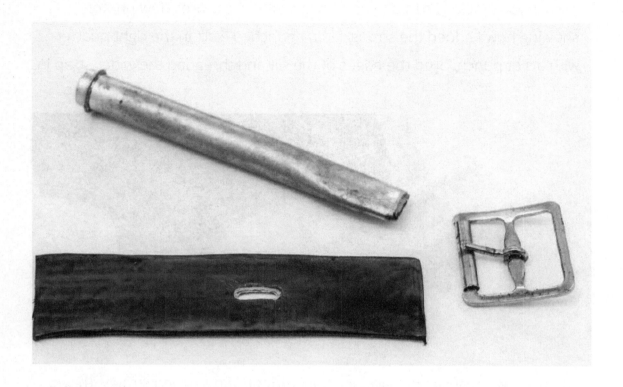

I then threaded the buckle into the strap, glued it together and secured it with a screw rivet.

Next, I punched holes in the strap in a square shape and stitched the buckle strap onto the quarter.

Suppliers

If you are on a budget, many tools can be found vintage or second-hand on eBay or Etsy, although it can be time-consuming to find what you are looking for this way.

UK

Springline

www.springline.net

Lasts manufactured in the UK. You can contact them by email and send them measurements of your feet or a drawing, and they pick the standard size lasts that best match them.

Leather & Grindery

www.leatherandgrindery.com

All kinds of soles, units and sheets, leather, recycled car tyre soles, Vibram soles. Also heel lifts, tacks and nails, shanks, adhesives (the whole Renia range), eyelets, Yankee Wax.

The Identity Store

www.identityleathercraft.com

Leather, tools, dyes, metal finishes. I especially recommend The Identity Store Leather Stain Collection with many colours to choose from.

A & A Crack & Sons

www.aacrack.co.uk

Veg-tan leather from Italian tanneries also the J&FJ Baker & Co sole bends, stiffeners, toe puffs and heel lift leather.

Osborne Leather Tools

www.hwebber.co.uk

Punches, awls and needles. I use their stitching awl, sewing awl haft No. 145 together with the coarse straight needle no. 413 N8.

Abby England

www.abbeyengland.com

Ritza 25 Tiger thread also leather, tools and general leather craft supplies.

George Barnsley & Sons

www.georgebarnsleyandsons.co.uk

George Barnsley & Sons were the world's largest producer of tools for the shoemaking industry, based in Sheffield. With the decline of traditional shoemaking, demand for their wares dwindled, which led to their closure in 2003. They still sell their tools from leftover stock. Their website is worth a visit just to look at the many different tools used in traditional shoemaking.

Italy

Buyleatheronline

www.buyleatheronline.com

Vegetable tanned leather for uppers, soles, midsoles and lining.

Guiardini

www.leatheredgepaint.com

Water-based leather dyes, edge dyes and top coats (gloss finish, dye fixative, leather conditioner).

USA

Sorrel Notions and Findings

www.sorrellnotionsandfindings.com

Lisa Sorrel is a boot maker with a very well stocked shoemaking supplies store. Lasts, leather, soles, tools, adhesives and more.

Shoedo

www.shoedo.com

Mainly bargain shoe lasts.

Brooklyn Shoe Supplies

www.bkshoesupply.com

Lasts, tools and other shoemaking supplies.

Rocky Mountain Leather Supply

www.rmleathersupply.com

Leather, high quality tools, threads, hardware, adhesives.

Tandy Leather

www.tandyleather.com

Tools, hardware, adhesive and more.

Canada

Londsdale Leather

www.lonsdaleleather.com

Lasts, leather, tools, nails.

Leather Wurx

www.etsy.com/shop/leatherwurx

Ritza 25 Tiger thread

Australia

Leffler Leather

www.leffler.com.au

Leather, tools, adhesive (including Renia Aquilim), hardware, soling and more.

Adelaide Leather and Saddlery Supplies

www.adelaideleather.com.au

Large range of hardware for shoe and bag making as well as some leather, tools and other supplies.

Tandy Leather

www.tandyleather.com.au

Leather, tools, hardware, adhesive and more.

Feedback

If you have any questions regarding shoemaking or would like to give me feedback, please don't hesitate to contact me at neda@secondskinblog.com.

People write to me in many languages, which is fine, I can use Google translate, but unless you write in German or Spanish, I will have to answer in English.

If you post the shoes and boots you made with this book on Instagram, please tag me @secondskinblog, I would love to see them!

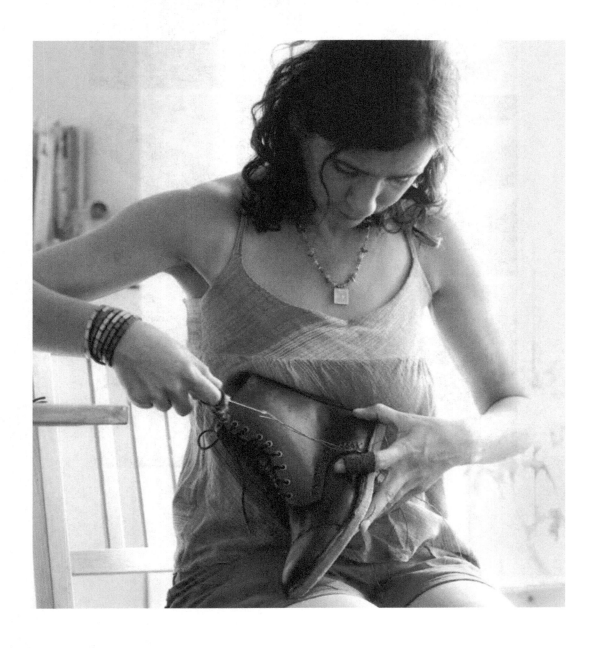

Check Out Neda's Sandal Making eBook

How to make unique leather sandals is a pdf eBook and can be found on my Blog www.secondskinblog.com

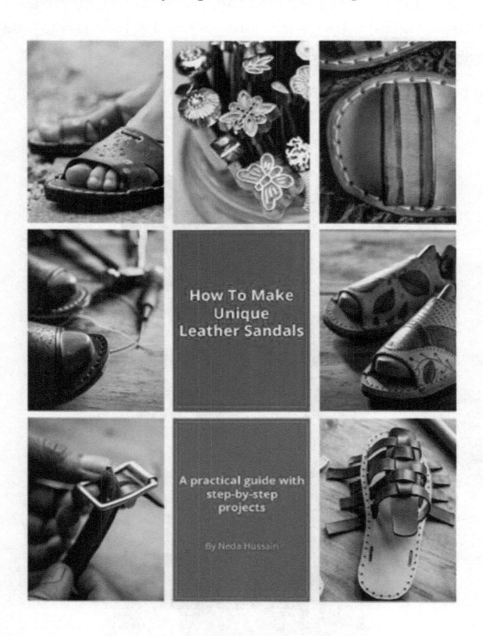

Made in the USA
Las Vegas, NV
25 January 2024

84873718R10136